TOVAH
MIRIAM

TOVAH
MIRIAM

A Non-Swimmer Considers Her Mikvah

—

On Becoming Jewish After Fifty

—ESSAYS—

MARY E. CARTER

TOVAH
MIRIAM

A Non-Swimmer
Considers
Her Mikvah
On Becoming Jewish After Fifty

Mary E. Carter — July 23, 2014

Mary E. Carter
ISBN 978-0-692-26582-6
www.Mary-Carter.com

A Non-Swimmer Considers Her Mikvah / Mary E. Carter

This memoir also includes some fictionalized stories based on
actual events and people.
Some names have been changed to ensure privacy.

TOVAH
MIRIAM

Published by Mary E. Carter DBA Tovah Miriam Gershom
www.Tovah-Miriam.com

Book Design: Gary W. Priester — Cover Photo: Shutterstock
Another book By Mary E. Carter:

Nonfiction
*Electronic Highway Robbery:
An Artist's Guide to Copyrights in the Digital Era*
Published by Peachpit Press, 1996

For Gary

—Contents—

Glossary

Bashert – a destined soul mate or something that is meant to be.

Beit Din – a rabbinical court that decides halachic questions and supervises conversions to Judaism.

Challah – traditional Jewish braided bread.

Charoset – a symbolic food which represents mortar; eaten during the Seder at Pesach (Passover).

D'var Torah – a lesson or a talk about a portion of Torah text.

Ger Tzedek – a true convert to Judaism.

Halacha – from the Hebrew root "to go or to walk"; the collective body of Jewish religious law including, but not limited to, Torah, Talmud, mitzvot and rabbinic decisions.

Halachic – according to Jewish law or Halacha.

Haimish – a Yiddish word that suggests unpretentious warmth.

Kippah –a Hebrew word for the Yiddish word, yarmulke; a skullcap worn in Jewish religious observance.

Kugel – traditional Jewish food; a noodle casserole.

Kvell – to feel happy and uplifted; a heartfelt feeling of joy.

L'Chaim – a Hebrew toast; To Life!

Lashon hara – halachic term for derogatory speech about another person. Lashon hara differs from defamation in that its focus is on the use of true speech for a wrongful purpose, rather than falsehood and harm.

Maideleh – a little girl

Mazel Tov – a Jewish exclamation of congratulations and best wishes.

Mezuzah – a case attached to the doorframe of a Jewish home which contains a parchment inscribed with Torah text.

Mikvah – a Jewish ritual bath used for the sanctification of a conversion and for other ritual purposes in Jewish life.

Mishpocheh – the whole family by blood or by marriage.

Mizpah – half coins worn to signify remembrance; Mizpah, a place in ancient Palestine where Jacob and Laban erected a heap of stones as a sign of covenant between them (Genesis 31:44–49).

Parsha – the Torah portion studied by Jews worldwide; each week all Jews study the same portions.

Parsha Lech L'cha – Genesis 12:1-17:27

Parsha Re'Eh – Deuteronomy 11:26-16:17

Pranah – a Sanskrit term for breath.

Rosh Hashanah – the autumnal commemoration of the Jewish New Year.

Shabbat – the day of the Jewish Sabbath; starts on Friday at

18 minutes before sunset and continues through Saturday until the sun sets.

Shanda – Yiddish word for shame.

Shiva – the seven days of mourning at the death of a loved one.

Shuckeling – ritual swaying during Jewish prayer.

Simchat Mikvah – a name that Mary made up for her own personal holiday in remembrance of her mikvah and commitment to Judaism. Simchat means a joyous event.

Tallis, tallit – a fringed shawl worn for Jewish services.

Yahrzeit – the annual observance of the date of a loved one's death.

Yom Kippur – in the Jewish high holidays this is the Day of Atonement.

———————

For more detailed information about Glossary terms and words, you may want to consult these online sources:

http://judaism.about.com/od/judaismbasics/a/What-Is-A-Kippah-Yarmulke.htm

http://www.jewfaq.org/index.shtml

http://dictionary.reference.com/browse/haimish

http://www.chabad.org/

http://thomer.com/yiddish/#Y

There is a story, always ahead of you. Barely existing.
Only gradually do you attach yourself to it and feed it.
You discover the carapace that will contain
and test your character.
You find in this way the path of your life.

—Michael Ondaatje, *The Cat's Table*

—Part One—

—Mishpocheh—

Pistol Packin' Mama

My mother and I played badminton in our living room when the summers were too hot in Southern California. She was a mean badminton player. With splendid athleticism, she lunged around the furniture, lobbing the shuttlecock with the strokes of a tennis pro. She had a fierce competitive focus that I believe came from her having been the middle, and the girl-child, between two brothers. As a cerebral only-child, I did not have the requisite fire in the belly for sports and so I was never a very serious badminton opponent for her. She spent her life trying to toughen me up. I spent my life daydreaming and wanting to be Van Gogh.

We tromped right over the backs of the upholstered chairs and sofa to get our shots—squashing pillows, tipping tables, crashing into the bookcase. I loved the teetering lamps, airborne hard candies, flapping draperies, the general delinquency and hysteria of it all. In our energetic exchanges, books flew and magazines slithered onto the floor. A glass candy dish met its maker, spewing its guts. My mother could not have cared less about damage to the things in our living room. She laughed uproariously as objects scattered and I would laugh too—she had a very infectious laugh—and we'd giggle, and hoot and screech as the game heated up. Yet, through it all, no matter how giddy we got, she played for keeps. She was going to win.

She smacked the shuttlecock smartly across the net. I ran all herky-jerky and lobbed it clean over her head into the dining room. We laughed and laughed and laughed.

Then one of us would call "king's ex" and we'd flop down on the nearest somewhat abused wingchair, breathless and sweating. There was not a thing in that living room that was not dislodged, scattered or scuffed. The room, our badminton court, lay in splendid disarray. Puffing, panting, then breathing more and more steadily, we would talk.

—If anybody hurt you I would kill them.

—Mama!

—No. I'm serious. Anyone lays a hand on you and I will kill them.

—But Mama, you'd be sent to prison for murder.

—I don't care. I'd serve my time and be proud of what I'd done. It would be well worth it.

This was not just idle motherly protectiveness. My mother, Mary Zimmerman, served in the United States Navy during World War II and was a gunnery instructor. She could dismantle, clean, assemble, load and fire with accuracy a wide range of military firearms, including air-to-air machine guns. In combat she would have been an ace.

She was up for Officer's Candidate School when she got pregnant with me and was finally mustered out in the spring of 1945.

Something was lodged in me on that hot summer San Fernando Valley day, playing badminton in the house with a mother who would not shed a single tear over a broken candy dish, but who would have, with unquestioning swift and very able anger, killed anyone who would have hurt me. And she told me so. Her legacy to me was her fierce beauty.

Written in 1944 when my mother was twenty-three and a gunnery instructor during World War II, this letter to her family was penned on United States Navy stationery:

Dear Family,

I'm amazed at how much I've learned in just a week —I can now strip a 30 cal. machine gun—I know how to operate a turret and guns contained in it...shoot a pistol and 12 gauge shot gun, run a trap house— compute various sighting problems—name advantages and disadvantages of various iron sights, telescopic sights, and reflector sights...also today we started a class in teaching methods...when the bill is passed in the House of Reps to allow Waves to go to advanced bases the gunnery instructors would be the first sent as they are considered the most vital as we not only instruct, but are prepared to run training devices that gunners must practice on as often as possible...
Love, Mary

THINGS THAT HAPPEN

ANNETTE SLUMPS ON HER SOFA, straining to sit upright,tilting to her right, ribs sinking onto pelvis. Just sitting there is a demonstration of her remaining athletic strength. She is a tennis champion. Now, reduced to bone and medication, she is at the end of lengthy, unintelligible and terminal medical babble, the wrap-up phase for yet another case-history that will be the record of yet another competent failure of an oncologist. She will die in a few days.

Under her scratchy and hot wig, her head is bare and veined. Her once robust gleaming cheeks are grey and damp this afternoon and her lower jaw juts forward, chin sharp, teeth in a rictus of grinning good sportsmanship. It is her birthday. Around the room are shadowy others—her sons, their wives, her brother, his wife, a niece, a nephew, someone and someone, and her old grey dog, one ear up and one ear down. Everyone grins following the suggestion of Annette's grin, in shallow, inane conviviality.

Here, you can see them all in this snapshot.

Through sinking nausea, Annette takes in the banter. She blows out the birthday cake candles, makes a wish—I wish I wish I wish I wish. Somebody, a shadowy tall man, her son, her brother, someone—he toots a toy horn and there is laughter, stupid and hopeful, and with no real hope at all.

Here's another snapshot. See the little toy horn?

The phone rings, earsplitting. Annette's son Gary picks up the heavy black receiver. He listens for a moment.

—This is Barnard. May I speak to my daughter?

Gary carries the phone receiver and winds its twisted black cord through the little company and hands it over to Annette. The receiver lolls heavily in her hand and she steadies it with her opposite hand. Gary steadies it too and says,

—Mom, it's your dad.

—Hello?

Blank. Silence. Nothing. Annette listens. The room listens, not hearing, not breathing. She nods, steadies the heavy receiver again.

—You call me now? You, you call me today?

It is silent again and she listens pressing her ear firm, her wig pushed up a little at her temple. She had had the most wonderful red hair.

—You call me today? After nothing—nothing!—for forty years?

Silent again, she shifts her body to sit up straight on the
sofa, pushing the coffee table with her slippered foot. Her
hand trembles and her knuckles stretch white with
gripping.

A moment more of silence and there is just the faint buzzing
of a voice from the other end of the line, then quiet. Annette
sits firmly up, not trembling any more.

—Where have you been for the past forty years when I
needed you?

And she slams the receiver onto the phone cradle with one
last lob of her muscled tennis stroke, skimming the net and
with all the accumulated power of her hard-focused, swift
return. Pock, she slams, masterful, in-bounds and hard. She
slams the phone, swift and final, down. And her opponent
is dead. Wham! She grand-slams the phone into silence. He
is dead to her.

With the echo of the phone pounding around the walls,
there are a few muted throat-clearings. Somebody says,
"Oh." A shoe scrapes the edge of the coffee table. Her little
dog limps over to her, struggles onto the sofa, rests his chin
on her lap, worshipful.

See him in this little snapshot? Always in her lap.

Annette: My belated heroine. You did so gracefully and so
completely what I never had the grit or strength of
character to do. You held your racket, kept your eyes on
your opponent's careening shot and slammed, hard as hurt,

with precision and practice. You slammed that ridiculous fuzzball with the intention of David, strong and decisive, and aced your last game. Love: One zillion. A stunning triumph. The crowd goes wild!

If only I had been more like you, Annette.

Things We Imagine

Because of the untimely deaths of both of our mothers, they never met. And neither Gary nor I ever met our respective mothers-in-law. We've talked about them over the years, wondering what they would think of Costco or the Internet or what they would say to us if we asked them to tell us all the family secrets.

Gary imagines the following scenario: We are sitting at home and there is a knock on the front door. It is our mothers, Annette and Mary, here to visit us in New Mexico in 2013. We answer the door and there they are: Annette with her tennis racket, Mary with her .30 caliber machine gun. They are here to join us for dinner, a short visit from their world—the world to come, as we call it here in our world. They have come back to see how we, their children, have turned out.

—Oh no, Gary! What would I cook?

They step into our lives, crossing our tile threshold, and into our great room. They nod vaguely at my huge paintings of guardian angels, the two of them, Annette and Mary, the embodiments, perhaps, of those winged figures that I had painted so long ago. And here they are, returning for a visit.

—I guess I could make chicken. Chicken is always okay.

We sit down in our kitchen, Annette leaning her tennis racket against the wall, Mary setting aside her weapon.

—Gary, this is weird.

They sit at our kitchen table smiling and sitting here, just a few ineffable degrees removed from us. They seem pleased, but they drift, floating up and down, as if helium filled. We are their children. They used to tuck us into bed. Now we are older by far than either of them had ever been in this world. And this new world, it is so confusing to Annette and Mary. It's noisy and everybody is staring into little TV screens all day long and typing and there are buses in San Francisco with signs that read, Use Condoms. What is that about? Mary and Annette bob back and forth in their chairs.

—What about baked beans and wieners? How about that, Gary?

We sit down at our kitchen table and look back and forth at them, first at Annette then at Mary as they drift around in front of us.

—Mama, look at me! I'm an old woman here. Look at Gary, Annette, he has white hair.

We just sit there, expecting something from them. The questions we would ask:

Why did you…

When did that...

Who was the...

It is silent sitting down to dine with Annette and Mary. They smile, vaguely in our direction, not really here, not really there, but courteous and ladylike, a little strained, perhaps. Conversation lags. Dinner sags, tepid. I made meatloaf and mashed potatoes—always good. Yet here we sit, Gary and Mary, all grown up now, sitting down to dinner with Mary and Annette.

Mary and Annette smile vaguely, nod to one another, pick up their things, no purses this trip, and without actually leaving us, Mary and Annette simply fade, going back to somewhere, back to somewhere that is not here. They are pleased with their offspring, the nice meal, the nice house, those nice pictures in the living room. What a nice older couple Gary and Mary are. Our mothers are courteous, appreciative, but fading.

—So nice, dear. Lovely evening, my handsome boy. Lovely meal, dear. Such a good little cook and so talented too. So lovely, yes.

Annette and Mary. Mary and Annette. Au revoir, until seeing you again, until re-seeing you both, bye bye.

Whoever is Here, Whoever is Not

Not with you alone do I seal this covenant,
but with whoever is here, standing with us today...and with
whoever is not here with us today.
—Deuteronomy 29:13

THIS IS THE STORY of how I splashed to the surface of the
waters of my mikvah, breathing my first breath as a Jew.
It is the story of how I came to step into those waters in
celebration and in continuity with Jewish life after I was
fifty. It is a story about how I contributed to the Jewish
diaspora by increasing it by one single individual—me!

If it is imaginable to have been somewhat Jewish by default,
I can honestly say that I have never missed a single yahrzeit
for my mother's death, September 30, 1968. But when I
started my annual observances, I had never heard the word
yahrzeit. Seventeen years would pass before I would learn
that word. Seventeen mornings I woke up and thought, it
was today, and, instead of lighting a candle, I had to go to
work. During most of my career I was an advertising
copywriter.

Sitting around the long corporate conference room tables,
reading aloud to clients and to account executives the TV

commercials that I had written—for dog food and for banks and for tacos—I would remember, with a twist of grief in my heart, that today's date was important, was horrendous. But on any particular September 30th, like all my other workdays, I had to go to work and to pretend to talk seriously about things that were not serious, were idiotic, even, compared to my personal yahrzeits. And I would think—as the executives around the table harrumphed through reams of marketing input—well, at least nobody died today.

Lately I discover that my story has the added pizzazz of being about a person who did something new and exciting later in life. The news is focused on my generation and how we are starting new ventures and going in new directions in our lives. Some are starting new careers. Some are returning to university to get doctorates. Some are breaking up long marriages and starting new families. My story is not organized around mission statements or business plans or curriculum vitae. Nor is my story about seeking or finding God. I will leave discussion of God to the rabbis for now. Perhaps later in my Jewish life I will consider God, but for now my story is concerned with the events and people that influenced me in discovering my new Jewish life. And, although this is not a how-to book, it could be helpful for anybody contemplating a late life change. And, of course, it may also add insight to anyone thinking of becoming Jewish later in life.

My story has happened, and it continues to reveal itself, through the unfolding events and actions and insights of a lifetime. I did a few things and a few more things until, seemingly suddenly, I did something which I could not have predicted earlier in my life.

I am a bit too old to be counted as a *boomer*, but much of my experience has been influenced by being born at the end of WWII and raised in white bread America. Being raised in the fifties had its own atmosphere – a mixture of toxic San Fernando Valley smog and our parents' smugness about their victory over the enemies of democracy. In that era democracy equaled stuff – washing machines, draperies, sofas, nice cars, green lawns. We lived in a culture that equated accumulation with wealth and wealth with success and all of that with contentment. Back then every parent in the neighborhood was a citizen-soldier now, transformed by their war experiences, blooming with confidence. Jobs and money were plentiful, even if housing was not. TV advertising focused our parents' postwar vision on the stuff they would come to need to create a safe and privileged environment for us little kids. It is no small coincidence that I sought a career in advertising. I saw so much of it growing up.

Decades passed. And then what happened?

When I splashed up from my mikvah and took my first breath in my new life I knew very little about what was to come. My rabbi had taught me that,

> At the moment you came up from the waters of the mikvah, as far as the tradition is concerned, you, as I, stood at Sinai. Literally and for real. But if you want to take that as poetry, try this because it isn't. At the

*moment you came up from the waters, all of Jewish
history in one instant became your history, the same
as if you were biologically born to it. Powerful stuff
all of this.*

And so with all of Jewish history now my own history, I
would need to dry off, get dressed and get going to discover
my own place on that long Jewish continuum. As I
considered my mikvah, I saw that I had never before
summoned the courage to plunge into a whole new life.
But this time, I was braver. This time I was ready to change
my life entirely. And I did.

How I made my Simchat Mikvah is contained in the
kaleidoscope of my life's events, occurring over a long
period of time and all jumbled together— kaleidoscopically
I might say—bits and pieces of my life's events juxtaposing
over, under, around and through one another.

Turn the kaleidoscope, either clockwise or
counterclockwise, and go forward or backward in time.
Someone from my past bumps into someone I met last
week. Something I learned in childhood bumps into something I Googled yesterday. This is Torah! After my mikvah,
I was again reviewing things and people who were *with us
today*…and the things and people who were…*not here with
us today*. After my mikvah, I began to see my world from a
new perspective.

The question to consider in my story is always this:

And then what happened?

A year after Gary's uncle died our Aunt B. struck a kitchen match and kindled a little white candle and I ask her,

—What's that?

—Today is the anniversary of Martin's death and this is a yahrzeit candle. This is how we remember and observe the anniversary of a loved one's death.

And that was it. If it is imaginable to have been somewhat Jewish by default, then that was me.

Jews do not proselytize. But the persistent student can find a way in. This is a funny kind of club, tight-knit and tight-lipped, proud and stiff-necked. Hey, do you want me or not? I write my story in deepest gratitude to those who show me how to be Jewish in the world. My Hebrew name is Tovah Miryam bat Avraham v. Sarah. So now already you know something about who I am. The rest is commentary.

Out of My Depth

WHEN I WAS A SKINNY LITTLE KID of seven I took swimming lessons in the San Fernando Valley. It was 1952. The swimming pool reeked of chlorine—its water was teeth-chattering, eye-dazzling neon blue. My swimming costume included a squeaking, rubbery bathing cap that smelled of old car tires and was so tight over my ears that I had what I call pool deafness that lasted throughout my swimming lessons.

We little kids wobble and shiver into the water as it engulfs our goose-bumpy stick legs. The occasional show-off boy rocket bombs right into the depths, setting off huge waves that splash onto our screaming, wavering little limbs. It is not remotely fun.

Our first lesson is: Put your face under the water and, submerged, blow your breath out. Big gurgling bubbles blub up under my swimming cap and fill my ears with a squeaky, rubberized glug. Water swooshes into my ear canals. I pop out of the water, deaf and breathless. I gasp a deep lung-full of the noxious fumes that make up our sunny California air. This idyllic substance is a stinging mixture of brown, breathable particulate matter (later determined to be toxic): incinerator smoke, car exhaust fumes, and atomic bomb-test fallout. I am strangled with a sore throat and burning lungs.

I pass my swimming test, if swimming was what that was, lunging and kicking along the side of the pool, holding my breath the whole length and popping up at the far end to receive my little swimming certificate. Everyone said that I had swum well. But I knew in my heart that I couldn't swim at all. For the next few years, swimming became clutching as I crabbed along the edges of various pools and, still later, swimming became sunbathing as I lounged on various Southern California beaches. My secret remained safe for decades.

And then came the mikvah.

Conversations of Palm Trees

Once upon a time, on a sultry 1974 Los Angeles summer night, with uncharacteristic thunder rolling in the distance, I am at a huge outdoor barbeque party. This is not a dream, though, looking back on it, there are dreamlike elements. The party, crowded and noisy, is hosted by the company I work for. This company produces photostats and halftone film negatives for the advertising industry. I am a copy camera operator and film stripper there. I am twenty-eight years old, three years divorced, owner of a faded tan Volkswagen with torn seat covers. I also own a refrigerator, a stove, a sofa, a double bed and a record player. I attend our company party alone.

My employer invites people from all of the major advertising agencies, graphic design firms, entertainment magazines, and newspapers in LA. These are our clients. Our periodic company bashes are legendary, oiling the wheels of commerce among formidably inebriated mobs of marketing mavens. During this party, this melee, this extended sales pitch really, I meet Gary. At some point in the reverberating rock and roll evening a friend of mine whispers to me the news,

—This guy's in *LOVE* with you!

—Oh, no! Spare me.

I am not interested. Am I?

—Who?

—He's over there. He's with the blond.

—Wonderful! He's with a date! Where?

My friend points him out.

—Over there. See. He's waving at you.

A little finger-waggle wave from across the room from him. He has sad eyes. He loves me. Pretty soon I discover I love him too. It was love at first sight. Near enough.

Love at first sight? How? Why him? Why then? Was it intuition? Probably.

Do you believe in intuition? I do. Some psychologists and scientists call this kind of flash of insight the *Aha Phenomenon* or the *Eureka Experience* and it's referenced in current psychology texts. These days the *Aha Phenon-enon* is being studied under controlled conditions, using MRI technology. But I have to say, in my experience, whenever I have had an *Aha* moment I am very far indeed from the nearest MRI machine, so how could anybody possibly study this ineffable thing in the lab?

It feels like it happens in my heart when it happens to me.

For me, an intuitive leap often has an accompanying rapid heartbeat and breathlessness. Sometimes when I experience an *Aha* moment, I giggle inappropriately. Science is now confirming my personal physiological reactions and researchers observe that intuitive leaps occur in the right hemisphere of the brain, sometimes with inappropriate giggles and rapid heartbeat. To me it feels like it starts in my heart.

It is the same way after many of my Introduction to Judaism classes. I leave class smiling as I walk to my car. Sometimes, inappropriately given the serious nature of some of the lectures, I giggle.

As an artist I float, fly or fall within the mysterious liquid interstices of the right side of my brain where wordless concepts pop up spontaneously. Inspiration, intuition, the spark of the divine, creativity, the subconscious, free association, the *Eureka* or *Aha* moments—call it what you will—this is how I function in my daily life as an artist. I am accustomed to working from my right hemisphere. Even in my career as an advertising copywriter, the best headlines pop into my brain without so-called rational thought.

So joining the Jewish diaspora is pure inspiration for me. It is a *Eureka Experience*, or a cartoon light bulb going off overhead. It is a pure *Aha* moment of existential relevance, and since I am accustomed to functioning with information from this mostly non-verbal part of my brain, I feel normal making an important life decision by observing my own reactions of rapidly beating heartbeat and giggles.

I leave class and go outside into the warm breezy evening. The sycamore leaves are rustling overhead and I know that I will do this.

In Talmud it is said that Rabban Yohanan ben Zakai did not leave unread

> *…the conversations of palm trees…*

So maybe there's precedent for my hearing something —what?—something that drew my attention to the dry sycamore leaves over the synagogue as I leave the building. Conversation between trees or an *Aha* moment or pure intuition, I will do this. I know that I will embrace the whole Jewish tribe. I will join my Jewish husband as a Jew.

CHRISTMAS TREE JEWS

NOT THAT GARY AND HIS FAMILY were particularly observant. My husband's family kept a strictly secular household. They had come from Russia and Lithuania before WWII, resided briefly in Leeds, England—where, coincidentally, my father was born—then went to Wisconsin and finally settled in the Beverly Hills diaspora. These Christmas Tree Jews exchanged gifts and phone calls on December 25th. Gary and his cousins attended, and sometimes even participated in, Christmas pageants that were part of their schools' normal course of holiday festivities. There were no Jewish holiday observances or days off in the Beverly Hills diaspora of that time. Gary's mother made pork and beans for her annual Christmas party.

The only thing Gary's family did Jewishly was to marry and bury with the rabbi.

But whenever a conversation turned to things religious, Gary always said, "I'm Jewish." Funny kind of Jew I'd say later. You don't do anything Jewish. And he would just shrug. When I first met Gary's Aunt B. she subjected me to a bit of casual lashon hara about my not being Jewish. She finally resigned herself to me with, "Well, at least you're Jewish by injection."

But get this: When we moved to our new home, retiring to

New Mexico, Gary suggested we get a mezuzah. With the combination of my having married into a Jewish family and Gary's sporadic observances, I had already begun living along the edges of a Jewish life.

But long before that, Jewish thinking, culture and history came to me from the influence of my mother. She had persuaded me to read *The Diary of Anne Frank* in 1958. *The Diary* was not part of the junior high school curriculum back then in the San Fernando Valley. But my mother wanted me to I read it, and we talked about it a lot. It was significant that I was fourteen when I read Anne Frank's diary and that Anne, too, was fourteen when she began it. Her diary was my introduction to the Holocaust and to the concept that there could be such evil in the world. My mother told me that some people are so evil that they do not have souls. She told me that Nazis didn't have souls. This may sound harsh or simplistic of her. My mother was anything but simplistic. She had a subtle and agile intellect. But she also had a directness that was, at times, shocking. I believe she wanted to introduce me to the concept of evil and that she would have realized that her description of Nazis was extreme. But I also believe that she wanted to show me, through Anne Frank's diary, that there were dangers and horrors outside of our little protected neighborhood. And, too, remember that my mother had a fierce protectiveness. After all, she vowed she would kill anyone who harmed me. It must have been excruciating for my mother to read Anne's words and to realize (as I did not yet at that point in my life) the evil that was perpetrated in the world that had forced Anne and her family into hiding. She knew that somehow she had to introduce me to this event in history and so she spoke with righteous rage as she informed me that there were people without souls.

Yet, even before *The Diary of Anne Frank*, my iconoclastic mother viewed the world in her own way. She was not like any of the other postwar San Fernando Valley mothers. For example, she did not have me baptized when I was an infant. She did not believe in infant baptism. She allowed me to attend Sunday schools with my little school friends, more for socialization than for religion—me an only child. And so I attended, occasionally, a few Protestant Sunday schools. I did this on and off—more off than on—until I was a teenager.

My family did not belong to a church and on the odd occasions when they attended services it was as if they were going on an anthropological expedition. My grandmother and one of my mother's brothers did not celebrate Christmas. No Christmas trees at Grandma's house. None at my uncle's house.

By the time I was seventeen I had read a potpourri of thinkers and authors, sometimes in school, often on my own. Plato, Thoreau, Hemingway, Freud, Sagan, Alcott, Steinbeck, de Beauvoir, Sartre, Friedan, Dumas, a little Buddhism, a little Hinduism. I was a sponge, absorbing knowledge with enthusiasm and energy, as much as possible, yet indiscriminately. That was between ages twelve to seventeen. Around age seventeen I drifted away from my San Fernando Valley Sunday school ethnocentricity and I asked my mother if the Buddhists and Hindus would all burn in hell for not believing in Christian doctrine? And she said to me,

—No. They won't.

We talked about this for a while and her words would echo later in my life. At that point, I quit Sunday school. After that I never attended chapel in college, never said grace over meals, never followed a guru or any other charismatic spiritual leader, and never joined a congregation, a zendo, church or ashram.

This Much I Know

His long legs scuffed up whorls of dust as he strode, quickly, quickly, bent slightly forward at the waist, into the wind, along the dirt road to Sophia's house. In his front jacket pocket was his letter of acceptance from the University of Illinois, Class of 1896. Never one to hesitate, Walter applied purpose to everything he did and much of what he did was to rush forward, maintaining forward motion, as he would say, legs as thin and graceful as willow saplings.

—Anna Sophia. Anna, Anna, Anna-Banana.

—Don't call me that.

She scolded him, teasing girlishly.

—All right then, Sophia. My beautiful Sophie Sophia.

Her head didn't even reach his shoulder when they stood together. But then those Zimmermans were tall folk. Walter had five inches added to his six feet. He never slumped. Wouldn't be right. He stood spine-straight, bony shoulders square, long slender feet pointing straight ahead.

—Let's get married, Sophie. You can go to college too. Dad signed the permission for us to get married and your dad will sign it for you too. And we can live upstairs in the rooming house across from campus. And you can study Latin and literature and you can be a teacher and I'll study engineering and I'll be a famous hydraulic engineer and work on dams and I'll patent my ideas too. I've already got my auto-tractor patented—well, as good as—it's pending, but I know it's going through. We can live in Chicago. We'll be happy. We'll have ten children. We'll be a family. We'll be us, Sophie, you and me! Say you will.

She couldn't look at Walter when he got like this. She shifted her gaze behind him looking across the hen yard, then across the fields, and she squinted, unblinking, into the dusty sunset.

—Walter, I…

He reeled around, pulling her down to sit beside him on her front porch steps. He folded like a jackknife around her side, grasping her little hands in his, and staring hard into her face.

—Sophie. Sophie. Beautiful Annie-Sophie-Sophia. Anna Sophia Morsch. Say you will marry me. Say you will.

And so they were married.

Walter found any old minister at any old church. None of those Zimmermans went to church. The Morsch people too, not much church. There was a little wedding meal at the

Morsch house later that afternoon. No time for pictures, but the couple looked happy. You could sure say that!

The Meyer family came. That was a scattered lot who lived with the Zimmermans. The husband—was it Henry?—he was never around, riding the countryside around LaSalle County, looking for land for a settlement of some sort. So the neighbors said. John Zimmerman and Henry Meyer made harnesses and farm tack. Had a little business outside Earlville. Did that for years. And now those kids, Walter and Anna. Everybody knew Walter was sweet on her. You could see him a mile away, scuffing back and forth from the Zimmerman's place to the Morsch place—went on all summer like that one year and she was just a little mouse of a thing. Sickly, so the neighbors said. And those Morsch children, one for each and every year for a decade and each one smaller than the last one and Annie the last one in that brood. European or German or something like that. Foreign. So the neighbors said.

Anna Sophia Morsch was Mrs. Walter Herman Zimmerman for nineteen years, and Walter did become a hydraulic engineer. He invented a system for automatically returning condensation from steam piping and headers and separators to boilers and auxiliary apparatus. Or something like that. Anna didn't really understand it all. Patent granted. Walter also patented a method of constructing dams and other hydraulic works and this would take them to California pretty soon. And they would go out there to see what's what and drive around, Ooh-ing and Ahh-ing as Walter called it, driving the empty dirt roads of the San Fernando Valley imagining everything —houses, orange groves, people, new towns—and all of it powered by water.

Anna Sophia, beloved of Walter Herman, died of kidney failure in 1912.

The first of this Zimmerman family of mine arrived in America around 1838. The 1850 census shows them living in the same house with a Meyer family. Most of what I have learned about the Zimmermans has been through the web site ancestry.com. The bits and pieces of the Zimmermans provide tantalizing clues, but not much concrete information about their characters, their beliefs, their origins in Europe. While I suspect that they may have been Jews, I do not have definitive evidence to prove that. The story about Anna Sophia Morsch and Walter Herman Zimmerman is my own fantasy about their lives based on where they lived—farming country—and some of the people in their lives. Searching for my Zimmerman roots has been time-consuming and, in the end, puzzling.

But here's a tidbit: Zimmerman or not, Bob Dylan is not my cousin.

Try as I might to make it so, the arbiter of all things genealogical, ancestry.com, says it ain't so. If wishes were horses, beggars would ride. That's what Grandma would have said. My mother was a Zimmerman. Bob Dylan's name was Zimmerman. All the wishing in the world can't make us cousins. His Zimmermans and my Zimmermans are not related. Darn.

—Here, you can have *Those Zimmermans*.

That's what Grandma said as she shoved two dusty old
photo albums into my arms. At age fourteen I had taken an
interest in my family history. Grandma had rummaged
through her old trunk and dug out the Zimmerman photos
and handed them over to me in her peremptory way. It was
the way she acted when flinging a dead mouse out her back
door. *Those Zimmermans* she had said, in her withering
tone. I knew that tone of voice. It was sensibly to be
avoided.

My grandmother, Jennie Myrtle, married that tall
handsome widower, Walter Herman Zimmerman, in 1914.
They had two sons, my uncles, and a daughter, my mother.
In later years she called him Zimmerman, and the whole
Chicago lot, if she ever referred to them by name, which
was almost never, she spat out as *Those Zimmermans*.
Impossible to know why. Nothing much was ever said about
Walter Herman during my lifetime. Not by my grandmother, not by my mother. If it were not for ancestry.com,
I would never have discovered my grandfather's first
marriage or the household the Zimmermans shared with
the Meyer family. Grandma never said anything about him
or them. It was as if they did not exist.

Gary, my husband of now almost forty years, looks at this
photo and remarks,

—He's Jewish.

I look over his shoulder at the handsome young man,
my grandfather.

—Why do you say that?

Gary shrugs and says,

—Because *all* the guys at Beverly Hills High School looked like him.

It was a tossed off remark on Gary's part. Still, Gary can be somewhat prescient in odd ways. This starts in me a line of thought. I spend several years wondering about my family, trying to sort out the people who I knew only as *Those Zimmermans*.

But the clues are sparse and inconclusive. I show my bits and pieces of evidence for my having Jewish blood to a rabbi. He studies them with serious intention, as if they were fragments of the Dead Sea Scrolls.

I come from a family of leavers apparently. By leavers I mean, people who leave, those who leave a place, a community, a family, a nation, who leave well enough alone, those who leave no trace. Leavers do not stay. Stayers stay, stay home, stay in their country of birth, stay in families, and stay in touch.

If *Those Zimmermans* were Jewish, then I have returned to being Jewish. If they were not Jewish, then I am the one who has left them.

The rabbi holds the photograph of Walter Herman Zimmerman, University of Illinois, Class of 1896. He studies it carefully and says,

—He's a handsome man.

My evidence for the Zimmermans being Jews is pretty thin, not conclusive enough for the rabbi to allow me to make a ritual return to Judaism. And so I will proceed with Introduction to Judaism classes and study with the rabbi for another way to join.

Walter Herman Zimmerman
University of Illinois, Class of 1896

—Maideleh—

IN PEACE, BORN

I AM BORN in the San Fernando Valley when it is dirt roads and orange groves. My mother waits out the war at my grandmother's ranch, pregnant, anxious, twenty-four. My father is in the Royal Air Force, away, somewhere, in danger. The scent of orange blossoms fills my mother's pregnancy. That free perfume must have made its way into her bloodstream and into my own cells as I float, a suspected twin, inside her comfortable encircling womb. As it turns out, I am a single, not a twin.

My earliest memory is visual, my new eyes receiving their first remembered images from about eighteen inches off the ground upon which I toddled. There is sunshine, white clapboard, a narcissus, an iris with strappy leaves rising over my head. Those memories acquire accretions over my lifetime as my mother gradually fills me in on her pregnant summer of '45. Grandma had hens, geese, a cow, fields of alfalfa, an apricot orchard. A letter from my mother, still pregnant with me, to my father, who was somewhere in the European Theatre, dated August 1945 says,

Thank God our child will be born into a world without war.

Two months before my birth the first and last atomic bombs were used to end a world *within* war.

Bohemians

When I was in elementary school I got an allowance of fifty cents a week. Payday was Friday and my mother always gave me two quarters. I earned this money by helping her with the dusting around the house and by bringing home reasonably impressive, though never quite brilliant, report cards.

Every Saturday morning my mother and father and I go to our local Thrifty Mart in the San Fernando Valley. And, while my parents maneuver through the produce and the abundance of the San Fernando Valley food chain, I dawdle around the comic book stand. Supermarket activities surround my comic book assessments.

Remember the screech of the saws from the meat departments in the fifties grocery stores? I never hear that sound these days in the sanitary and bloodless shopping pavilions where I load up on food and toilet paper. These days I never see a piece of meat that actually evokes a whole real animal. When I was little, whole and half carcasses of cows, pigs and sheep swung from hooks right out in the open behind the grocery store meat counters.

Huge men whacked and sawed at the animal remains and thumped and hacked them apart on cutting tables where our mothers would supervise. These butchers wore long-sleeved white lab coats and utilitarian bloody aprons and, on their big bloodied palms, they displayed the naked cuts of meat for our mothers' approval. They wrapped your chops in butcher paper—thump, bump, bump—caressing the brown paper tape with their enormous powerful swollen knuckles. I do not remember anyone, young or old, ever turning away or even flinching at this daily mundane carnage.

At the comic book rack, I look over the week's fresh new offerings. Every weekend there are new comic books to covet. I love Nancy and Sluggo best. What kind of a name is Sluggo, I wonder now? Nice Jewish Boy, perhaps? It never occurred to me back then. Nancy and Sluggo had round perfect heads and diminutive front features. They were not exactly cute, but their looks passed my mother's careful scrutiny as characters with whom it would be okay for me to practice my reading skills. I had an intuition that Nancy and Sluggo were somewhat down-market so I felt I was getting away with something, just a tiny bit, by reading their adventures. My mother was omnipresent in her zeal to protect me from the dangerous influences and the subversive color schemes of...

Bohemians—making them, of course, completely fascinating for me. What-the-heck was a *Bohemian*? I wondered. Were Nancy and Sluggo Bohemians?

Interestingly, my mother did not have that common mother's horror of comic books. On the contrary, once she had flipped through them and assured herself that they were Bohemian-free, all she ever said was,

—Well, I'm just glad you're reading!

The saw in the meat department shrieks as it dismembers another dead cow and I gather up my weekly haul, Nancy and Sluggo on the top of the pile.

Veg-O-Matics and Voice-Overs

I STAND AT A WORN GREY REDWOOD FENCE with a hose running cold water, a skinny little kid on a very hot day in the summer of 1953. It's the San Fernando Valley, hot with smoggy choking air, and it is perpetual summer. I'm standing in front of our side-yard fence which separates our little tract house lot from our neighbor's little tract house lot. The whole neighborhood is checkered out like this, little new houses with identical floor plans and identical backyards and identical fences corralling us little kids into our own bit of this measured landscape. Straggling along our fence is a purple trumpet vine, intended to cover the utilitarian property line with lush flowering beauty. But it's too hot for the vine to gain a foothold and the dirt between our blacktop driveway and our neighbor's blacktop is too hard and sparse and probably too toxic and the poor little vine wilts without hope against the old wood fence. I am doing the voice-over for a TV commercial. I am eight years old.

With TV brand new in our living room, I watch the *Mickey Mouse Club* and *Ramar of the Jungle* and *Queen For A Day* and Art Linkletter's *Kids Say the Darndest Things* and *The Cisco Kid* and *Father Knows Best*, all of them interspersed with TV commercials. I like the TV commercials the best. I love the product demonstrations:

Veg-O-Matics with voice-overs and a camera that moves in
to show a woman's disembodied manicured hand, pumping
up and down, thunk, thunk, thunk, easy as pie, graceful as a
dove, chopping celery and carrots and onions—onions that
won't even make you cry with your miraculous *Veg-O-Matic*.

So when I go to play outside, I play TV commercial. As I
drag the hose over to the redwood fence I put my thumb
over the nozzle to form a perfect arcing spray and I do the
voice-over demonstration showing how my new miracle
product will paint your old fence without harming nearby
plants. I pretend that, for the fence, the product acts as
protection to cover it with a beautiful new color. But on the
plants, it acts as harmless water. I spray the whole distance
of the fence as I chirp,

—It's quick. It's easy. And it's harmless to your plants.

FRENCH ONE

I READ EVERYTHING. Reading becomes my habit. With some books I am sad when they end. Sometimes I thought I would never find another book as good as the one I had just finished.

Not long after my comic book days, but very long indeed before I knew what any of it meant, I read a paperback book at Grandma's house by Francoise Sagan called *Bonjour Tristesse*. At thirteen years of age, I knew by the instinct of the pre-teen that this was something big, something important, and something I might even be getting away with. My mother probably did not see me reading it and, although I was not a sneaky child, I was cautious. I, a Nancy and Sluggo graduate, sensed that *Bonjour Tristesse* should be protected from my mother's scrutiny.

As I read it, I sense also that *Bonjour Tristesse* features Bohemians. Grandma does not seem to mind my reading *Bonjour Tristesse* at her house. I'm sure she sees me reading it, skinny legs draped over the back of her sofa. Sagan was only eighteen when she wrote *Bonjour Tristesse*. As a teenager I recognize the voice of a contemporary, though dimly, through my social ignorance and through my San

Fernando Valley smallness. Sagan speaks to me, though faintly, across our cultural schizophrenia. She evokes tristesse—a concept I have no hope of understanding at thirteen. With my gym bag and my French One, I am sure that I get only the vaguest sense of what her book is about. Yet Sagan communicates a visceral kind of torpor in me.

In her book, Sagan introduces herself to me. She is a French teenager, a foreign teenager, and yet she understands and writes about concepts that I don't understand yet—and what a strange portent reading her book would turn out to be for me—strange foreign concepts way beyond my innocence and years, very *je ne sais quoi*, for a little girl growing up in the San Fernando Valley. But I want to be like her.

After Nancy and Sluggo, there was not much that had prepared me for reading about subtle angst and Gallic ennui. But with a kind of woozy dawning instinct, from my cozy, hot-summer San Fernando Valley, I absorb *Bonjour Tristesse*. Without knowing or understanding her book, but nevertheless knowing and understanding it by a whiff of intuition, I want to live a life that includes ideas that are subtle and thoughtful and—what?—I could not have uttered a single intelligible sentence about what *Bonjour Tristesse* evoked in me back then, living my little life, a very protected daughter in the bright new landscape of little stucco houses on nice little tree-shaded streets. As a San Fernando Valley teenager I did not yet know how to aspire to critical thinking, but I had begun to experience the mysteries of my own intuition.

THOSE BASTARDS!

(A Message in a bottle)

Dear Dad,

*I am sorry that Grandma was so impossible when you
finally got home after the war. I am sorry she kicked
you and Mama and me out. I am so sorry that this
happened to you and to my mother, leaving you alone
in the night with your military uniforms and arm
patches, citizen-soldiers, both of you, of the good war,
refugees now, rewarded only with that universal badge
of courage: an outrageous mother-in-law.*

BUT. BUT GRANDMA ZIMMERMAN was a wonderful grandma
for me. She took me very seriously and talked about grown-
up things with me. She even taught me how to drive.

Gripping the steering wheel of her black Chevrolet two-
door, her freckled hands at ten and two exactly, her legs
extended straight out in front of her, she takes me for a
spin. We lurch backward, Grandma looking over her right
shoulder. Then she shoves the shift stick and we jerk
forward, whiplashing a little. She deftly recovers control of
the vehicle by shifting fast into first. We are going forward

now in a nice graceful little skid around the blacktop turnout. Down the driveway front-ways and just a little bit too fast. And so my lesson begins:

—The fundamental principle of driving a car, Mary, is to maintain forward motion.

And off we go.

Grandma had a job. Nobody's grandma in our neighborhood in the fifties had a job. And it was not just a prissy grandma job, either. Grandma was a linotype operator. She took me downtown to see the ghastly basement machinery at the newspaper: huge, black, clacking machines with hot lead dripping into little troughs and the printer's ink sinking into her fingerprints and men swearing and Grandma swearing. I learned how to swear from Grandma, did you know that?

One sunny San Fernando summer backyard afternoon I am playing with my neighbor, a skinny little kid named Tommy and his dog Rags, spinning round and round, Rags biting and snarling at one end of an old blanket, Tommy and I doing tug-of-war on the other end. I don't know what made me to yell at Tommy,

—You Bastard!

Mama hears me from the kitchen and comes to the back door waving me inside. This very instant! She sits me down and starts to lecture, on and on and on, as mothers do and ever will continue to do, in unintelligible motherly scorn and righteousness, on and on and on she holds forth, me her only, and squirming, audience.

I endure her long and steady lecture, her words and concepts and her ideas on social acceptability and what is right and what is wrong and all of that and more and more and way too much. Finally she asks me her singular mother's question:

—WHERE on EARTH did you LEARN to TALK like that!?

—Well, gee, Mama, Grandma calls EVERYbody a bastard!

What does a mother do with a child like that? With a grandmother like that? With her own mother like that? She can't help but laugh. And, laughing, says,

—Well, don't call any more of your little friends bastards.

—But Grandma…

—Never you mind Grandma!

—Okay, Mama.

And what I'm really thinking is,

—*Well, I'll never say bastard around Mama again!*

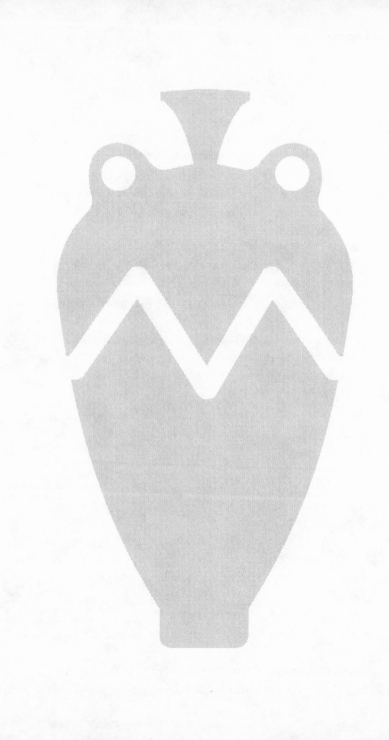

Aquarium Mirror

THERE IS A TROPICAL FISH AQUARIUM perched on a shelf in the waiting room of my orthodontist's office. It has a mirror on the wall above it and the mirror and anybody who looks into it, is illuminated, from chin upwards, by the bright green light from the tank. The water laps around as the fishes swim about and bubbles gurgle upward out of an aerator tube. The fluorescent green light leaps around my face in watery agitation whenever I look into the mirror.

Today I am thirteen and my hideous braces are about to be removed. Today my friendly torturer, the orthodontist, tugs at my hardware and one by one he snaps each ring off and flings it out of my mouth with a little clank into a metal basin. Then he cleans my teeth and I am done—the ordeal is over at last. I run my tongue over my molars and two front teeth and they are smooth like teacups. I pick up the little appointment card from the lady at the desk and go out and stand in front of the fish tank to view my watery reflection.

I smile. I am pretty. This is news.

As a small person with a little skull, my permanent teeth had bulged over my lower lip and distorted my upper lip into a Mortimer Snerd caricature—an English face run sadly amok. But now—now I am pretty. It is very big news to my little psyche. My mother is sitting in the waiting room and she smiles and I smile and I believe that she is relieved that this is over, my orthodontia.

I wonder if my mother had a little pang that afternoon, seeing me come out into the waiting room without my braces, a pretty little thing at last: Well, there she goes! Now I had a face that, not only could a mother love, but, too, that someone else might love. That has to feel like trouble to a mother, no matter how pretty her little one is at last.

BOOTS, BACKWARDS

I WAS A FRESHMAN in college. I was just leaving the science
building after zoology class, holding my notebook and the
big zoo textbook against my chest and this kid runs across
the quad yelling,

—The president's been shot! The president's been shot!

I run back to the dorm and up and down the hallways radios
are blaring and I hear Walter Cronkite say,

—President John Fitzgerald Kennedy was shot at 12:30 this
afternoon and died at 1:00 p.m. in Dallas, Texas, today,
November 22, 1963. The president is dead.

In the dorm girls are wailing in the hallways, crying and
screaming and hugging one another and kneeling on the
brown linoleum hallway floors, embracing and crying, and
I am crying too, a kind of retching, uncontrollable crying,
and girls are wailing up and down the hallways of our three-
story dormitory.

Then suddenly we are somehow in the dining hall—I do not
remember walking or running there, but suddenly we are
there—and the radios blare out over the public address

system, very, very loud in the recreation room and in the dining room and it is more and more news of the same news. Nobody eats lunch. The kids—we are no longer young adults on this day, but children again—we are frightened and lonesome and serious and we listen and listen and we look into each other's eyes and see reflected our own despair and a nauseating betrayal, too, which is new in our guts this day in 1963. Nothing was right in our world that afternoon. Nothing would ever again be right in this kind of world.

Somehow I got back home. And we watched the television for four days straight.

A riderless spirited horse, with black boots facing backwards in the stirrups, edges sideways, crabbing along the Capitol Hill road with slender equine beauty, black and out of context for our lives as we sit watching television. The riderless horse is shocking, dark and slightly out of control, as we are about to be. This thing happened. It is the first major political event of my little life. Frightening, political and jarringly personal.

On and on and on the story goes and we watch, our little family of three, the same as thousands of other little families, all of us diminished and our eyes stuck on the flickering ambiguous television screen with our stomachs in a knot—sick, sick. I am nauseated and, at just eighteen years of age, I experience a new form of tightness, a repressed angry taste of bitterness in my belly.

But worst of all, as I have discovered lately when I see the endless loops of that bit of television news from way back then—worst is my memory of the dark sound of the cadenced drumbeats that beat and beat and beat along the now silent parade route. The black horse and the black boots and the drum beating. Finally the television announcers shut up for the drumbeats and the crowds on the street shut up for the drumbeats and we all shut up in front of our television sets. I can still hear the drumbeats today in my head.

Nothing would ever again be right in this kind of world. The grown-ups had all gone berserk.

BELMONDO

FAINTLY, AND AT FIRST SUBCONSCIOUSLY, I hear the weird humming of a theremin as it drifts around the close harmonies of the Beach Boys' *Good Vibrations*. It is 7:00 a.m. on a school day at a small private university where I am now a senior, majoring in art. My white plastic GE clock radio is turned way down low so as to not wake anyone else in the dorm. The dorm has paper-thin walls which preserve visual privacy but do nothing to preserve us from shouts, giggles or blaring radios. As a senior this year, 1967, I know and abide by a few, a very few, remaining rules and regulations and courtesies. Waking up to a soft radio is one of the last dorm conventions I still follow. *Good Vibrations* is the theme song of that year.

A British dress designer, Mary Quant, has influenced skinny girls of my age to the point where we wear little dresses with hems that stop at mid-thigh and white fishnet stockings and shoes with square toes and square short heels and thin straps in the shape of a "T" with little brass buckles on the outside. Dressed like this today, I stand in front of my mirror and tease the hair on the top of my head until it stands out in all directions like a free-floating mad spider's web, and then I smooth down a carapace of my front hairs over this rat's nest and draw the whole thing back into a low ponytail which I fasten with a rubber band.

Into the stem of my ponytail I insert a big yellow polka-
dotted silk bow which is equipped with a straight bobby pin
that pokes into my neck a bit as I arrange it into the perfect
Carnaby Street doll that I have created. I comb down my
bangs until they line up perfectly with my eyebrows and the
effect is complete.

Good Vibrations has been replaced with Mic Jagger singing
about how when you get what you want you lose what you
have. I sling on my yellow slicker raincoat, which is a soft
marshmallow-y shiny bright yellow vinyl and not very able
to provide warmth today in the cold rain because it is
unlined and it is very short, ending just a tick above my
dress hemline—but who cares. I stand in front of the full-
length mirror outside my room and sway back and forth
and pout like Twiggy. Maybe, since it's raining anyway, I
might exchange my clunky shoes for my red mid-calf boots.
This I do, and off I go to the art building.

I can honestly say that in 1967 two tracks rubbed along in
my mind. First, was the boyfriend track, currently occupied
by that silent cigarette-smoking painter—Belmondo as I
call him. Second was art and, excruciatingly, how I could
cut the class that was currently giving me the most trouble.
Figure drawing from the live model was impossible. I saw
the work the other kids were doing and it was so much
better than my work. I hated failing. I hated looking stupid
in front of the other kids. So I cut that class often in the
beginning.

Our teacher showed us a human skeleton one day—we had
to trek over to a biology lab to find a human skeleton—and

he told us that this skeleton was that of a female human being. He moved her bones gently and delineated with his long fingers the arch of her iliac crest, like a lover, like a connoisseur of bones, he showed us how that curve of bone pushes from beneath the skin which stretches over it to form that delicious semicircle that we see from the outside as the curve at the top of a woman's hip. I have always remembered the part about the bone pushing from beneath the skin. We were to feel it there when we drew from the model. I do not believe that I knew how to feel that bone when I drew it in 1967, but I do now.

It is a way of drawing that involves sensing the bone from inside my own finger tips. It is the feeling of holding my pencil at a certain angle and pressing it around some mental image of the iliac crest and its skin. And it involves making this gesture a thousand times in drawing after drawing.

Belmondo of the art classes. On the first day in figure drawing we mounted our drawing horses and Belmondo, arms folded provocatively across his skinny tee-shirt chest, fastened me with the gaze—you know the one, you know that gaze—and I fastened back and it was love.

Love?

Again. As usual.

He was the putative bad kid. I was, well, if not wholly innocent, then certainly a bit simple. Be it ever thus, eh? Perfect! Just perfect—it was—after all, it was the sixties,

the absolute perfect time for sex, drugs and rock 'n roll.
You had to be there, you really did. And I was. And so was
Belmondo.

He had a name of course, his own name. But perhaps he is
still alive and it was all just so ephemeral and lovely and
stupid. I will let his name rest. I let his name rest just in case
he has a personal liability attorney in his employ, along
with his staff of personal assistant, personal trainer,
psychotherapist, and/or wife, grown children and/or
delusions of grandeur enough to cry "Libel!" Or, maybe,
just maybe, he now resides in San Quentin.

I used to have such a fantasy when I shopped at the mall in
Larkspur and I would look up and see the prison walls off
in the foggy Marin County distance, and, as I passed the
chic stores, I would wonder if he had become a drug lord
and ended up, skinny and dangerous, on death row. In such
a fantasy, he might still have had the clout to have me
disposed of if I used or slandered his real name. And so,
Belmondo.

Our college had a provision within the university regulations that allowed for kids who were caught smoking
substances, or disturbing the peace, or otherwise whooping
it up, or acting unruly, to be taken to the campus police
instead of to the town police. None of this youthful
stupidity would end up on one's permanent record. The
worst that could happen was that the miscreant would
receive a lecture from the dean and it was possible that the
kid's name would go onto a kind of dean's list in reverse —
not the one for the outstanding student but for the student

who stood out for bad behavior.

Those were simpler times.

In the protective atmosphere of a small conservative
university, far from Berkeley and Bohemians and fire bombs
and actual bloody violence, we were allowed to be curious
and uproarious and moderately law-breaking at times and
the softly delinquent among us, when captured, would
receive a mild tut-tut from the college authorities.

We sit on mattresses on the floor of Belmondo's bedroom
with all the roommates and their girlfriends gathered
around, sitting tailor-style, waiting for our turns with a
substance-filled hookah and listening to records. The
Rolling Stones and Bob Dylan. We listen to Dylan's *Sad
Eyed Lady of the Lowlands* and wait for our turn with the
marijuana. The hookah was a bit of exotica that came from
Cost Plus in San Francisco. A metal mouthpiece was
attached to a long flexible pipeline, attached to a metal top
that could be removed when water was added to a glass
reservoir at the bottom. This last item looked like a flower
vase, and it probably had been in another retail
incarnation. I am unclear on where the marijuana burned.
But burn it did and the smoke somehow went down into the
water and we sucked it up the flexible cord and passed it
around the room to one another.

I am not too clear on all of this, but I believe we would stop
up the mouthpiece with a thumb as we passed it around so
as not to waste any of the valuable marijuana smoke—
thrifty little souls that we were, we clean, middle-class kids

and our thrilling vices. We were suitably nervous and paranoid about our smoking activities, and Belmondo took great pains to close all the windows and doors, lock them and pull the shades down. There was much elaborate preparation and much pulling back of the shades, just a crack, to check and double check that "the feds," as Belmondo called them, were not in the driveway. From outside the house, I imagine that none of this shade-pulling and peeking and re-peeking escaped the notice of the neighbors. Surely we were not fooling anybody. Maybe the neighbors were smoking, too. It was the sixties and we were very paranoid.

And yet, we were such a baby bunch. It was just a little bit before the extremely hairy period of the sixties, or, rather, because we were college students at a very conservative university, we could only go so far in the externals of our junior rebellions. We were somewhat still under the thumb of our parents; we had to go home every few weeks for inspections and haircuts. *You'll get that haircut, boy, or you'll break your mother's heart! Do you know what she's been through?!*

I have a snapshot of myself with another of those painter boyfriends of that time. This boy's father had blood pressure you could watch in his neck when he got onto the topic of his son's hair. This man sputtered, yelled, admonished and even bribed his son to cut his "gawdamnedhippyhair." The snapshot I still have shows a very ordinary lad with very ordinary hair. He had thick black hair, but, though longish for its time, was positively clean-cut in light of hair styles that were to come in the

next few months. And you know what? You can guess if
you give it a little thought. This boy's father was stone bald.

In 1967 I ride the Greyhound bus to San Francisco. With
as little knowledge of what was being created across town
at the City Lights Bookstore as I had had of the subtleties
of *Bonjour Tristesse* a few years earlier, I came to San
Francisco solely to shop. Dilettante, poseur, what I wanted
that cold sunny day was shoes.

I walked from the bus station south of Market, across the
street and uphill slightly on Powell to Union Square, Macy's
and Joseph Magnin. There was a shoe store on the corner
of Maiden Lane and the shoes I wanted were there inside
that leathery smelling heaven—little white shoes with short
square heels and the charm point was that they were bound
in an outlining stripe of black. They were small and deeply
fashionable and cost the earth at $35. Astonishingly
expensive for that time—well, for me at least. My college
allowance was $70 a month, cash money.

We did not have credit cards in 1967. I would peek in my
wallet and count and re-count my bills and coins, planning
my other purchases and only fretting a little bit about
having enough for lunch. Lunch would be a hot fudge
sundae at Blums. In addition to those shoes, I also coveted a
dress over at Joseph Magnin. I left the shoe store with my
handle bag and jostled and wove through the other women
shoppers to cross the intersection to Magnin.

Joseph Magnin had the most beautiful full-page ads in the
Chronicle and the *Los Angeles Times*. These ads were

rendered in an extravagant baroque Beardsley style of
flowing opulent pen and ink lines. Each ad featured a
single, arching, skinny-leg girl in a tiny-morsel shift dress,
glittering with pattern and curl, the girl blinking out at you
with big fake feathery eyelash eyes and swirling paisleys of
black eyeliner. These lush illustrated dollies purse tiny black
morsel mouths at the reader and speak volumes.

You are not good enough. You, you teenage consumer with
your ratty hair. You, who looks at me, you are simply never
good enough. Forget those shoes you just bought. They are
hopelessly out of style this minute. They are out of style
because they become so the minute you purchase them.
Silly girl. Foolish girl. But look at me. The man who draws
me makes me unreachably thin and arrogant and fashionable. Even as we tempt you, we mock you.

So, oblivious, I go off to Joseph Magnin, impoverished,
slightly awkward, with my forty remaining dollars and my
return bus ticket back to the dorm. Joseph Magnin smells
like a perfumed scarf in a tiny leather bag strung on a strap
sewn with pearls. It is money. I melt into the escalator and
ride up to heaven where skirts and dresses hang, lank and
alluring, on abundant roundels.

The dress I covet is black, short—very short—double-
breasted with white plastic buttons the size of fifty-cent
coins. These white buttons are sewn into place with black
thread and go from the boat-neck rolled collar at my
clavicle down the front to the last button at the middle of
my thigh. At $35, it is a dress to be reckoned with. This
dress is made out of black cotton which is woven in such a

way as to create stripes, shadow stripes. It is completely lined in silk. Well, no, perhaps not silk, really, not at $35. I have the luck of the draw, a body which displays clothing well. So it's hard to find anything wrong with the dress as I view it in the three-way mirrors.

On the bus I have my Joseph Magnin bag and my shoe bag and I am filled with ice cream and hot fudge and peanut crumbles and I have three dollars in wadded bills and coins left in my purse.

For the unformed late-teen with money, the images of Carnaby Street were worse than drugs. The intoxication was to have its way with me. I cannot honestly say that to this very day I have been clean and sober from the consumer drug of lavish female department stores, clean of the false promise of the little dress, sober after the seduction of the perfect shoe.

You can see where all this might have led.

If only—*only?*—things had been different I might have simply matriculated, graduated, married, borne children, worked, perhaps decorated a nice ranch style house in the San Fernando Valley, loved my grandchildren and eventually died—well, died, okay—having done the best I could possibly have done. Biology is destiny. Geography is destiny. My birth into the San Fernando Valley of orange blossoms and dirt roads points to comforts down the line. The calculus of this accident could have made me into someone very different, into someone much smaller than would have been possible had not 1968 come along. And let's not be coy, had not death come along, so untimely, into my predestined little life. Little, with the smallness of domesticity, is what my life had been before 1968.

In 1967 we lived in parallel worlds and it was called a family. But how much do children know about their parents after all? And how can a parent, busy, preoccupied, know a single thing about a child whisking along on that other track? I believe that the people in the world about whom we know the *least* are the very ones with whom we share the *most* biologically.

I miss her, I really do.

I miss that girl who went back and forth to art classes and shopped in San Francisco and had handsome silent painter boyfriends and didn't have to worry about the consequences of her mistakes. I miss the *me* who had nothing much to worry about at all.

Marlboros and Marijuana

THAT'S THE WAY IT WAS in 1967. And some rhythm track, a gentle little brush-on-cymbals riff, like leaves rustling, quiet and gentle and hypnotic—that little repetition would push forward into my hearing until it was the entire song—until it replaced Bob Dylan's lyrics and his electric guitar and I could not hear anything else.

The kids in the boyfriend's room disappeared and the smoky ambience in that darkened room disappeared and the bubbling hookah disappeared and all that I could hear, *all* that I could focus on was that little brushing, leaf-rustling sound mixed way back in *Sad Eyed Lady of the Lowlands*.

> *With her existential ennui,*
> *I aspired to be*
> *Anouk Aimee.*
> *A Poem by Me.*

It was glamorous to allow a boyfriend du jour to believe that I was her, Bob Dylan's sad-eyed lady of the lowlands.

Yet, there were flashes of the future that resided in us back in 1967. Like a flashlight scanning cave drawings, bits and pieces of each of us were illuminated during those sixties college years. The flashlight skims the strange drawings on the cave walls, here revealing a lion, there revealing the imprint of a human hand.

My mother and I shop during the college summers and holidays. She drove, me in the passenger seat. We loved to shop at Robinson's and Bullocks, snazzy upscale department stores in Los Angeles.

—I've been reading about the kids at Berkeley, she said.

—Uh-huh, I respond.

—I hear they smoke marijuana.

—Uh-huh.

—Do kids at your college smoke marijuana?

I was not a lying child. I started fidgeting.

—Uh-huh, I said.

—Do you know kids who smoke marijuana?

—Uh-huh.

This could be bad. She grasped the steering wheel of our Chrysler. We drove on for a few miles. Her mind was ticking over, I could tell. And, not being a liar, I was wondering about what pre-verbal answer I could summon at her next question.

But she never asked it, the next question: *Do you smoke marijuana?*

And off we went into Robinson's and bought patent leather shoes and a green shift for me and a floral shift for her and drove home.

The skinny rangy lads got drafted, some of them, and sent to Vietnam. One of them, or one very much like one of them, became a colleague of mine when I was in advertising a decade later. His eyes held mine, pleading and darkly defensive. He could not or would not talk about what had happened and yet his clothing—a khaki safari jacket and faded jeans—told a lot about him. And so did the way he moved through the corporate hallways, along the edges, lightly touching the walls as he went. He scanned everyone and everything along that hallway, which was a city block in length. He could not or would not join the banter and bitching in the creative department. His eyes darted amongst us, nervy and suspicious. He was one of the skinny boys of 1967 working as a copywriter in 1977. He fights for democracy in the jungles of Vietnam and democracy rewards him with a job where he flogs product in the corporate jungle. Ironic, his eyes. Frightened, those eyes. They held my gaze from behind a screen of Marlboro cigarette smoke. They fascinated me with their deep and empty silences.

If I had been IQ smart and street stupid, and if I had been pretty in a Carnaby Street sort of way in 1967, there would also have been illuminated a few sketchy figures on my own prehistoric cave walls. Sad, something really sad, was going to happen to me pretty soon, within just a few months. I had put on existential angst in 1967 because I had seen it in a French movie. It was glamorous to allow the boyfriend du jour to believe that I was her, that *sad eyed lady of the lowlands*.

At graduation, in alphabetical order, stoned and mildly hallucinating that the tassels on my mortarboard were bouncing spiders, I am seated by one of my boyfriend's roommates. Matt. Clutching his diploma he turns to me and says,

—Well, Mary-E, what are we going to do now?

Two months later he is dead. Dead as if he had gone to Vietnam—dead, but without the jungle. Silent beautiful boy, a lumbering bear with a black beard, he snoozed during the warm lectures of art history and left campus for days at a time. Then he'd come back and not talk to any of us. At least, he never talked to me. So I knew almost nothing about him except that he was kind to me. Maybe his kindness and his silence exuded something deep and mysterious. Or maybe he was silent because he just didn't give a shit. I mourn him, still, and wonder about him.

So there we were in June of 1967. Be-capped, be-gowned, newly diploma-ed: We knew everything about nothing. I had had no pain as yet on that graduation afternoon. San Fernando Valley born and raised. White bread, white parents, white-washed. I can't say there was much, if any, pain in my life at that point in 1967.

But my future was circumscribed already on graduation day
in 1967. I could not have known, or anticipated then, that
my life was in the countdown before genuine pain would
hit. Ten, nine, eight, seven—the countdown was at three
that day. I was at the conclusion of the cosseted portion of
my little life. The only pain I had suffered in my own
history up until that moment was the pain of inappropriate
loves, those skinny boys of 1967, and the pain that I put on
like a fuzzy sweater because it looked and felt sophisticated.

In just a few months my life would change. Life was about
to shovel it out to me and there would be no letup for me
anytime soon.

This is the end my friend.

I have wished, in all these subsequent decades, that I could
have re-captured, just for a few moments, some of that
lovely innocent nonsense. I have often wished I could have
been allowed just a single moment to stop saying to myself,

—Well, at least nobody died.

Everything About Art

PLEIN AIR PAINTING in May of '67. I take my paint box and canvas into a ploughed field near my college to paint a landscape for my oil painting class. Across the field I hear noises and shouting. I quit my painting to take a look.

I see across a muddy paddock a single muddy cow culled from a pen. I see her shoved inelegantly into a huge emerald green restraining machine. It has long metal vertical fingers the thickness of drainpipes. These utilitarian fingers clamp around her waist and with a loud clang she is trapped. I see a veterinarian wrestle her head up and sideways, shoving something down her yawning pink throat. I see another veterinarian use a kind of speculum to shove something into her soiling buttocks. Then, with a great clang and metallic screech, the green fingers spring apart releasing the poor crazy bellowing creature. She leaps, frantic, blind, twisting and kicking backwards, bucking away from her strange abduction, mud and excrement flying off her hocks. Bound in her machinery, she is suddenly released and she escapes, a wild beast, clumsy, medicated, puzzled, and crazy, bucking with bovine screams of indignation and fear.

—Yahrzeit—

1968 Now? Or Now?

A BLUE BOWL with a peach, a banana and an apple waits
on the desk by the window which is open to the hot still
summer air. Shimmering heat sulks outside the windowsill.
She is a skeleton, backlit through her nightie, hobbling back
toward me from the bathroom. I am so frightened. Don't
cry. Don't cry. You told me not to cry when I was with her.
My knees are knocking—they actually knock when my
heart beats jagged like this. She perches on the edge of the
bed, and then droops over sideways and lolls onto her back,
eyes closed, her lips compressed. She is the color and
texture of tallow, like melting candle wax on this hot
unbearable August day. Will it be now? Or now? Or now?

I kneel beside her bed. Now I lay me down to sleep.

Oh god, oh god, oh god!

Godless, I pray.

I kiss her arm.

You've Had a Nurse at Home?

When I graduated from college in 1967, I was an art major, a pretty good painter, a pretty okay person living a small, sheltered life, with a potpourri of great readings under my mortarboard and not getting into very much trouble. And then my world changed utterly.

There was no hope at all that my mother would survive her illness. None. The doctor said her chances were, "Nine months max."

Hospital assistants wheel her back to her room, after a truncated exploratory operation. No hope at all. She is still sedated and fusses a little at the jostling activity of people moving her from a gurney to a bed. I am dressed in a short plaid wraparound miniskirt and I have pulled my hair back into a neat Carnaby ponytail. We already know at this moment that there is no hope whatsoever. Still. Still the doctor will treat her with poison and burning. What for? This would not change a single thing about her illness; that it would kill her, and soon, was quite evident when they cut her belly open to take a look and sewed her up again, lickety-split, with no hope. There would be denial and a gauzy kind of hopefulness in the weeks to come, but I knew. I knew it because they had told me so.

She lies there in her first hospital bed and she looks young. I see that somehow she has suddenly lost her deep suntan and freckles. Her arms had been extravagantly spattered with freckles and now her freckles are gone. We lean in toward her as she lies there on the hospital bed. I stare at her arms. It is a shock for me that her freckles are gone.

I find my car in the hospital parking lot, unlock the door, slide in, and drive slowly and carefully away from the hospital. I drive carefully away, looking both ways at the intersections, carefully, easing up to stop signs, looking left, right, and left again. Driving mindfully down Los Feliz, I scream. My voice thuds, undramatic, muffled by the car seat upholstery and the wooly headliner of my car. That was the only time in my entire life that I had ever screamed. I drive away, driving safely, cautiously, as I drive away from that first part of my little life.

My father tells me that he and I will take care of her. I am to do days. He will do nights. He'll pay for my apartment and expenses and I am to quit my job— the first real job I had after college. And we do take care of her, just the two of us for the next five months, and then she dies.

On the afternoon of her death, I went to the hospital to see her. I discovered that she was in a coma. Nobody had mentioned that to me, nurses too busy I suppose. A candy-striper was adjusting the sheet. Back in 1968 young women volunteered at hospitals and they wore pink and white striped uniforms. Candy-stripers were high school age or maybe college students who were studying to become nurses. This girl, very much a doppelgänger of myself, looked straight into my eyes and said,

—You've had a nurse at home?

It had never even occurred to me. But, then again, not a single family member or friend had called to offer help during my mother's illness. I was so stunned by her diagnosis and so shocked by its effects that I had not realized that not hearing from anybody was not right.

I sat by her bedside that hot summer of 1968 as she died of stomach cancer. Washed her hair. Made her little trays of food. Kissed her arms. Shaved her legs. Do not cry in front of her. Do not talk to her about how serious her condition is. I had my father's instructions and I followed them. Dutiful daughter. And so I would go downstairs and cry into the guest bathroom towels, then go back upstairs and lie down next to her on the bed. I was twenty-two. I had been an art major in college. I had never seen someone so sick in my life and this someone was my mother and her illness was frightening in its virulence.

It would take twenty years for me to realize that not having a nurse was not right, not even safe, for her or for us. Twenty-eight years would pass before I discovered an old Xerox copy of a letter to Grandma that my mother wrote just three weeks before she died. In it she said, "They take such good care of me. They are like angels." It would take forty years for me to appreciate the hard honesty of being told that there was no hope for my mother. It would be ten years before I would paint again.

After my mother's death, my life would never be the same. I would never be the same.

Forgot About Today

I sat by the bedside of a man who had been a member of the Long Range Reconnaissance Patrol in Vietnam and who was dying at age fifty of non-Hodgkin's lymphoma from the hidden effects of Agent Orange, a defoliant which had been lavishly sprayed onto both the jungles and the soldiers during that conflict. And what seemed to be true is that, even in the last moments of his short life, constrained by the landscape of his bed, he wandered that jungle again, living again and again those events which would, pretty soon, kill him.

He held his arms in front of his hospital gown and his heaving chest, in the gesture of holding a weapon overhead while wading through water, and he asked me, panting and delirious, gesturing with his head to somebody—to nobody really—off to the side of the bed, "You like that guy? You trust that guy?" and so fought his last Vietnam encounter from that hospital bed in Connecticut. May his memory be a blessing.

Since the Vietnam War I have had several friends who were veterans of that conflict. As I suspected, they experienced worse things in that war than what I experienced in my life during that same period of time, back in and around 1968.

The veterans of Vietnam I know—now in their sixties, review that jungle war in private and secret moments, in the night, sitting in a favorite chair, reviewing, reviewing, seeing and seeing everything again and again.

You name it, and its name is always horror, its legacy is always grief.

My discovery is this: The bad things that happen during a human being's twenties become the formative events in the synapses, never to be forgotten and upon which will rest—for better or for worse—the whole psyche of the person who experienced them. Witness the veteran of war—the veteran of your war for example—witness that veteran at nine decades of age. He goes to tears describing his buddy who blew up right in front of his very eyes on Omaha Beach when he was twenty-two. It is as if it were happening again, right now, in front of the fragile, wrinkled, little ninety-two year old sergeant. These things are not forgotten, nor should they be. They are perversely comforting in their familiar pain.

Bad things that happen in our twenties stick and are formative, oftentimes formative of a much better soul than would have evolved had they not happened. Ironic, this.

So, too, I live, again and again, those events which would, if not kill me, would kill a certain part of me for a certain part of time. Bad things perpetrated by unthinking or capricious gods onto the souls of as-yet-unformed human beings in the first decades of life last forever and may never be undone. Neither therapy nor time can ease those pains inflicted early on in a life. Am I right?

As I say, there are worse things that can happen to people. Grief comes at you. Mine, relative to assassinations, atomic bombs, incursions, concentration camps…relative to tsunami, to hurricanes, to earthquakes…and certainly relative to kidnappings, hangings, murders, gunshots in the night…and relative to jackboots that strike…my grief was—relative to the wide variety of hells on earth—my grief was pretty small. My grief was only personal, only universal.

The stories of death that I have heard since I was twenty-two are instructive to me, each in its own way. Perhaps it's because there is this taboo against talking about death. Maybe this is the very reason that people are so urgently drawn to do so. There is a kind of perversity to this need to talk about something you are not supposed to talk about. But. You gotta get this dog off your back, and you can't do it in silence. Eventually the urge to say something about it will be just too irresistible.

I would imagine that death ranks as one of the top five reasons why people seek talk therapy: birth, death, marriage, divorce, sex. We are so limited in our ability to grasp death that, as a poor second, we can, and must, talk about it. And the taboo against such talk serves only to make this need more intense.

I am not much comforted by the person who says to me,

—There, there. Everything's going to be okay.

It is *not* going to be okay.

Okay?

Even my own mother used to say,

—This too shall pass.

I don't hold much with that world view. It *won't* pass. In fact I do not want it to pass. I want to live it, whatever it is. I no longer want to forget it. To go about my business as if nothing were, or had been, wrong. Wrong? That barely hints at it.

My favorite song lyric in 1968 was Bob Dylan singing,

>—*Let me forget about today until tomorrow.*

Somehow that advice, that lyric, got seated in my brain during the months when my mother was sick and dying and I took, quite literally, its advice and forgot to consider the impact of my mother's death on my life for the next eleven years. Well not exactly: I did not forget a single thing about her illness and death. But I soldiered on with my life as if something quite manageable had just happened to me.

Again I think to myself:

> *If it is imaginable to have been somewhat Jewish*
> *by default, I can honestly say that I have never missed a*
> *single yahrzeit for my mother's death,*
> *September 30, 1968.*

It was not only imaginable, it was a fact. I was already, in some ways, acting Jewishly by intuition and with intention. I observed my mother's yahrzeits, year after year, long before I even knew what a yahrzeit was. Later I discover that being Jewish is not about belief, it is about action.

I did not simply believe in a yahrzeit observance—I did not even know what the word meant. I had not even heard of the word. I was *making* yahrzeit. Yahrzeit was already instinctively a part of my being, of my psyche, long before I learned the word yahrzeit. There may have even been an element in my thinking that I had invented this little ceremonial observance, all on my own, instinctively. I was already giving life to my first Jewish actions.

—PART TWO—

—Rabbis—

It's Not About Belief, It's about Action

MY EXPERIENCE WAS THAT of the old saying: When the student is ready, the teacher will come. I had slowly readied myself by reading and I had had a couple of desultory conversations with Gary's Aunt B. asking her what she would think if I started to study with a rabbi. Her response was always,

—Think of the food!

She liked my cooking and probably envisioned challah and charoset and brisket coming out of my kitchen.

What is required of the student who wants to join the tribe? Classes, reading, thinking, questioning, discussion. And action. It is incumbent upon the student to find a rabbi to study with. Yet, knowing nothing, where do you find one?

In 1996 I attend a ten-day silent Jewish meditation retreat conducted by Rabbi David Cooper and his wife, Shoshona Cooper. Rabbi Cooper is part of the Jewish Renewal Movement and a student of Zalman Schachter-Shalomi, z"L. The retreat includes about two hundred people. There are about a half-dozen rabbis in our group.

We learn continuity practice for meditation—a kind of
walking, moving, daily minute-by-minute form of prayer
which is not praying with hands clasped, but prayer as one
walks and cooks and feeds the cat. Continuity practice
includes listening to trees. It touches me more viscerally
than going to services in buildings. We learn to observe, in
silence, the sanctification of *all* things—the sweet blueberry
tucked into the cake of a warm muffin, the susurrations of
leaves overhead, cool dew on our bare feet. We read Parsha
Re'Eh Deuteronomy 11:26-32 and Deuteronomy 14:22-29,
and each of us prepares a D'var Torah. We each are called
to read our pieces to the entire group on Shabbat.

Rabbi Cooper called us, one by one, to sit beneath his tallit
as we read. He showed me how to use a corner of the
fringes to point to the passage. For my D'var Torah I
considered the verse Deuteronomy 14:29:

> ...*the stranger, and the orphan, and the widow,*
> *Who are inside your gates, shall come, and shall eat*
> *And be satisfied.*

Here is what I wrote at that retreat:

> *I am somewhat a stranger—a metaphorical*
> *orphan—when it comes to navigating a mystical or*
> *spiritual path. I realized this on Thursday. For the*
> *first time in my life—and I am fifty—that not a single*
> *person in my or my husband's family has taken or*
> *had taken this route. Not my mother, nor father, nor*
> *grandmother, and not my husband, nor his parents,*
> *nor his aunts, nor cousins. Nevertheless, here I trek.*

Thank you for taking me, the orphan, inside your gates to eat and be satisfied.

When I get into my car and onto the freeway to go home from the retreat, I notice that all the traffic is whizzing past me. I think, well, there must be some sort of emergency behind me or up ahead on the freeway. I scan the road in my rear-view mirror. Nothing. Then I glance at my speedometer—I am going 40 MPH! The continuity practice of driving home!

So by the time that I had accepted the invitation of a dear friend to be her guest at her congregation's Rosh Hashanah services, I was ready without really knowing it. And in walks my next teacher. The Rabbi is haimish and had an open countenance. Later I would discover that he is learned and kind. I knew, instinctively, that he was the right teacher for me as I approached the moment of my mikvah. It was a pure *Eureka Moment* which was to have reverberating life consequences for me.

I love the fact that Jews do not proselytize. I love this about Judaism.

Rabbis teach a series of Introductory Judaism courses. Then, if one or two students ask for more study, the process seems to slow down. There might be a tradition—or is it just an urban myth?—that a student will be turned away three times. Also, it is understood that no member of a congregation will encourage the student one way or another.

Similarly, if one married into a Jewish family, as I had done, no family member will try to persuade you to join the tribe. It is a private act of will and conscience for each individual student. Jews make it difficult for the stranger in this strange land, even though Torah says to welcome the stranger. Ambiguous, but perhaps this form of obfuscation or seeming indifference to one's attempts to get into this taciturn group may be the first lesson:

One: You will be turned away as a Jew.

Can you take that? Can you take rejection from the world? Can you take rejection even from your own landsman? If you are not orthodox enough, can you take the rejection of the Orthodox? If you are not liberal enough, can you take rejection of the secular? Can you take rejection from the Nazi, the Inquisition, the plainly ignorant? Can you take rejection from the world—from Iran, from Sudan, from Alabama, Kansas? Can you take rejection from anybody—from a classmate, from a cousin, from the door-to-door missionary? Can you tolerate the intolerable? Can you tolerate the intolerant? Can you take the rejection of the anti-Semite? This is important. Fail this lesson and you might as well pack it in. To be a Jew, you need spine.

Two: you must always act—and much action is required of your own free will.

Nobody will entice you to join the tribe. You have to make your own decisions, think your own thoughts, and question your own motives. They make it hard. You have to study, to read. Nobody tells you how many books may be required.

You are thinking about joining The People of the Book.
Have you read enough books? How many books are you
willing to read in order to learn? How many books are you
prepared to read for the rest of your life? And it isn't just
reading. You must question and probe those books. As a
Jew, you are duty-bound to study and to question, to parse,
to analyze, to dissect everything you read. Do I have the
stamina? The integrity? The intensity? The intelligence?
This isn't easy, nor is it supposed to be.

On the first day of class, Rabbi says, and I write it down in
my notebook,

—Being Jewish is not about belief. It is about action.

> *It is not incumbent upon you to finish the task.*
> *Yet, you are not free to desist from it.*
> *—Pirkei Avot*

You are never too big to sit on my lap.

PRAYING DOUGH

MY MOTHER TAUGHT ME her pivotal truths. For example, she taught me that I had a guardian angel. She was unequivocal on this topic and through repetition, the concept stuck. She taught me that I could be or do anything I put my mind to, which over the years proved to be only partially correct, but I appreciate, nonetheless, her bestowing upon me that confident idea.

I learned these concepts—and countless others—either at her knee or on her lap. And she told me that I would never be too big to sit on her lap.

There was nothing equivocal about my mother. Things were what she said they were and that was that. This was often hard to live with. She and I butt heads over my wanting to go to Art Center College. I wanted to be an artist. She wanted me to get a university degree. According to her thinking, art would not prepare me for life, a bachelor's degree I could fall back on. We sparred back and forth for a couple of years over that one. I got the BA from a university. In Art. The BA was in my back pocket. Art prepared me for life...or for nothing. My graduation from college was to be the penultimate thing that I did to make her happy.

During my short life with my mother we talked constantly, analyzing, parsing and trying to grok just about everything. I asked her questions and she asked me questions. The most important question I ever asked her is worth repeating,

—But Mama, what about all the Hindus and the Buddhists and all the people in China who might be good people, living good lives—will they burn in hell if they do not accept Christian doctrine?

That was my question to her when I was seventeen. And she answered me with another of her pivotal truths and this one would truly turn my head around. She looked me straight in the eyes, her beautiful and intense brown eyes fixing on mine, serious and compelling, and said,

—No. They will *not* burn in hell if they are not Christians. It doesn't work that way.

Those words reverberated inside my head and inside my heart and I was set free. If a pivotal truth is one which turns one around, then it was that one that allowed me to, not only turn, but to take flight. I am not sure I knew, at that very moment, the profound effect my mother's words would have on me. But, from the vantage point of many decades, I understand the power of her words on me that day. My mother set me free to think for myself, to think outside of boundaries, to think creatively, to ask difficult questions, to explore, to learn, to change, if need be. I was set free by my mother's unique intellect and by her fierce individualism. For me, she was the embodiment of the woman of valor, her words far above rubies. What a gift she bestowed upon me. How brave she was!

Decades later I start to study, to read, I attend a Jewish
meditation retreat, I begin to take classes. I meet a rabbi.
He is both learned and haimish.

I meet with him in his office and we talk.

—Rabbi, I can't pray, I said. It feels like I'm asking Santa
Claus for presents. I can't sit in the congregation and pray
and feel anything other than foolish and phony. Other than
that, Rabbi, this all makes perfect sense to me.

And he said to me:

—Perhaps it's a question of your iconography, Mary. What
do you see in your mind's eye when you attempt to pray?

—I see the bearded old man with his finger extended on the
ceiling of the Sistine Chapel. No, I am not Catholic. That
image comes to me from years of studying art history. That
and the man on the cross and the blond lady with the halo.
It's all so extreme, made to make people afraid—I mean all
those bleeding wounds of Christ and St. Sebastian. You
know? Those are images to inspire fear and guilt. It is art
made to control people. It is brilliant advertising. That I do
know. It's pure manipulation by imagery. If that's all there is
to religion, I'm not made for religion. And most certainly, I
cannot pray without feeling like a hypocrite. Praying would
be hypocritical if I tried it with those images in my mind.

And Rabbi said to me:

—So it is a question of your iconography. Are you willing to read a book about God? More precisely, a book which talks about many very different conceptions in the iconography of God?

Another book to read. Of course I will read it: *Finding God*, by rabbis Rifat Sonsino and Daniel B. Syme.

If you want to join this learned tribe, you must read many books. Nobody tells you how many may be required. The books seem to self-reveal as you go along, which means that the minute you read one book, it suggests a topic or reference to another book, or two, or three, and you read those and the next books reveal themselves as being urgent and necessary for you to read, and so the list of books grows exponentially. This growing list never stops growing.

And so I read and read and read, the books squashing into my bookshelves all jammed into rough categories or stacked in groups of related topics.

Later I take Rabbi's Challah Baking class. Rabbi had us meet in the congregation's kitchen, a huge space with restaurant professional stoves and equipment and vast countertops and enormous kitchen mixers the size of small automobiles and pots and pans you could float in, right out to sea.

Rabbi enters the kitchen wearing an apron over his usual dress shirt, slacks and kippah. He has a timer, a kitchen scale, a pen-thermometer and a pile of papers: recipes, the history of challah, essays about the sanctification of bread in Jewish ritual and photos of various challah-braiding techniques.

Rabbi instructs us that we should weigh each individual ingredient on the kitchen scale. Nonsense, I think. I will measure the flour the way my grandma measured it—fill the measuring cup to overflowing and use the back of a knife to scrape off the excess. I will measure as I have always done. And for the wet ingredients, again he suggests measurement by weight, each ingredient done separately. I will, instead, pour the oil into a cup first, then pour the honey into the oil and eyeball their levels bending at the waist to see the red lines on the cup. Oil first, then honey. That way the honey slides right out of the glass measuring cup without sticking to the sides. Grandma had her ways.

Other than the differences between Rabbinic instruction (and a man's way of working in the kitchen I might add—tools and gadgets and technical precision) and my own way of measuring—slovenly by comparison perhaps, but learned at my grandma's side—the focus of this bread-making workshop is the braiding. Braiding dough I had never done before. Rabbi demonstrates, working the dough deft and quick. He has beautiful hands, Torah hands, accustomed to handling sacred objects. His loaf is done in three or four graceful moves. With reverence, he gently places the braided loaf onto the baking sheet to continue its rise.

We each get a ball of dough and a place at one of the kitchen's long stainless steel counters. A toss of flour onto the surface and we start. I take off my rings and place them at the back of my bit of ledge. I love that the dough resists my touch. It feels like a breathing creature, which, in fact, it is. It silently shrinks back as I roll three balls into fat ropes. Then, pinching my three dough ropes at one end, I braid—over, across—across, over—folding the pinched pieces underneath the finished braided loaf. A loaf.

While our dough is rising a second time, Rabbi goes over the history and lore of Jewish bread making. He explains why and how to toss a bit of dough into the oven and offer a blessing for the baking of the bread.

After Rabbi's challah class, he came up to me for a quiet word and said,

—You say you cannot pray in the sanctuary, Mary. But watching you braid your bread I say to you, *that* is your prayer, *that* is prayer for you. Don't worry about what goes on in services—just let the words roll over you if you become confused by them. Continue to make your bread and that will be your prayer.

My Loaves, My Prayers

—Patriarchy—

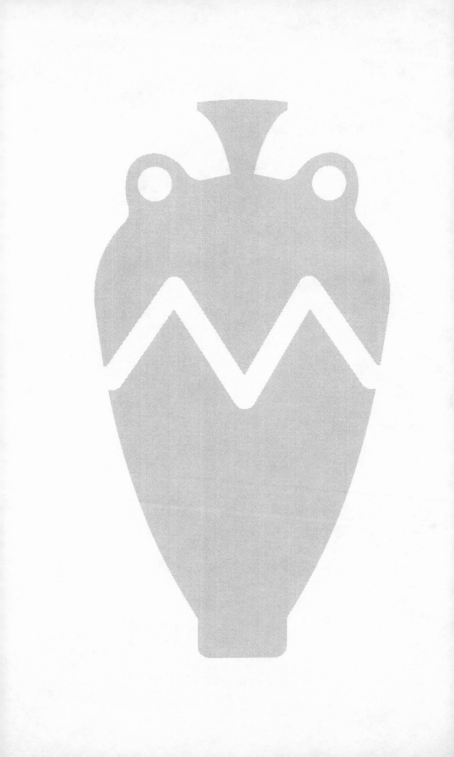

LECH L'CHA! GET GOING!

As a TEENAGER I fainted at every movie theater in Los Angeles—the Wiltern, the Paramount, the Chinese and the Egyptian. Waiting in line for *Ben Hur*, for *Gone with the Wind*, for *The Pink Panther*, for *Lawrence of Arabia*, I fainted.

My mother was an elementary school teacher so she and I shared all the school holidays. Summer was for the movies. Standing in line with my mother, on our long hot summer vacations in L.A., I would first feel a wave of panic, a woozy feeling in my belly and a ringing in my ears. Then a hot flush started in my body like a wave at the beach lapping up my legs and arms and I knew I would have to sit down or that I would drop down. Not wanting to disappoint my mother, and, really, really wanting to see the movie, I would try to wait it out, breathing in, breathing out. In. And out. In. Out. But it never got better. My vision would darken around my eyebrows as sparkling spots of darkness circled in my eyes. Then cottony deafness and voices receded. Softly, slowly, I would float into what sounded like a bed of cornflakes. I was never injured, protected by the oblivious looseness of my limbs in my fainting free-fall.

Then suddenly, surprisingly, and very loud, I would hear my
mother's alarmed voice near my ear,

—Mary. Mary!

Then she would get mad.

—You're not eating properly!

And I would protest,

—But Mama…

She would push aside the other moviegoers in line and rush
me into the theater lobby for a Snickers. Then we'd sit in
the cold lobby, side by side on old red velvet couches, bare
summer sleeveless arms touching, breathing in the buttery
smell of popcorn. We sat there recuperating, me wobbly
and picking at my candy medicine. Then she'd start.

She'd regale me with one of her longish speeches about
proper nutrition, about always starting the day with a good
breakfast, about vitamins and especially about the lack of
enough calcium in my diet. And then she'd change tack ever
so gracefully and observe how hot it was, really too hot,
anyone could have fainted in that heat and how the box
office had not opened on time so we'd had to stand there
too long and how it's no wonder that I had fainted. And
suddenly she was on my side, defending me against all
reason because that's how she was. Quickly her mind
turned around. That's how she never found fault with me,
but with circumstances. And with me still nibbling my

candy bar, but starting to perk up, we'd decide that, yes, I felt better and let's go in and find a nice cool seat and enjoy the movie. Which we inevitably did.

The landmarks of my childhood: the Wiltern, the Paramount, the Chinese and the Egyptian. Not the Hollywood sign perched and crooked up on that historic hillside. Not the iconic palm trees along the California streets, but places where I had fainted. Those were my landmarks.

I introduce them here to demonstrate and to personalize *Parsha Lech L'cha*, Genesis 12, which is what we are studying this month. It contains God's instructions to Abraham:

> *Go forth from your land, your birthplace, your father's house, to the land I will show you.*

It can be wrenching to leave your birthplace, your land, your father's house— literally, to leave those places, those personal landmarks. How poignant are the images of home even if they are somewhat peculiar, like fainting in movie lines. My personal icons of home include those movie theatres where I received my mother's comfort and support. This is not an easy instruction to act on. Yet, in this phrase is contained the sanctification of the act of leaving one place and going to another. It is a positive direction, given by God to Abraham. In order for Abraham to discover the land God will show him, the deal is this: Abram and his entire family have to leave, to even change their names.

To me, this Parsha is almost a mitzvah. It is certainly a mitzvah in the connotation of a worthy deed. This is an instruction that was to set the course of Jewish migration from one place to another, from that distant time of Abraham and Sarah right up to today. But there is a blessing here too. Perhaps a blessing in disguise. By moving from their lands, birthplaces and fathers' houses, Jews have oftentimes, and quite literally, saved their own lives. Hidden in plain view, this mitzvah of Abraham and Sarah can become the beacon for one who flees in fear and in danger to get to the border of the safe haven. Going from Spain to Portugal, from Europe to America, from Germany to Israel—these were ultimately life-saving escapes. And the blessing was, and still is, life! The blessing comes in the new lands.

Yet *Lech L'cha* can also be the words of sanctification to anyone who starts a new life, in a new place, with optimism and enthusiasm. My husband's grandparents fled Lithuania, settled in Leeds, chose a new life in Wisconsin and thrived in Beverly Hills. Their initial flight led to life for their children and grandchildren.

I am not the only student of Torah who takes this meaning from *Lech L'cha*. In *The Torah A Modern Commentary*, Rabbi W. Gunther Plaut observed that,

> *For while Abraham's story must be read as the biography of an individual, he…is more than an individual. The Bible sees the Patriarch as the archetype who represents his descendants and their fate. He is the forefather, whose life hints at the later*

> *history of the people of Israel. This prefiguration*
> *begins when Abraham becomes a wanderer. Time*
> *and again his descendants will wander across the*
> *earth, along the highways of history.*

Here is another example of leaving a life to create a new life:

The words of *Lech L'cha* are of particular poignancy, to me, to my own life. *Lech L'cha* speaks to the person who flies, not fleeing in fear, but with arms fully extended, to embrace the entire Jewish tribe. Making this journey requires, absolutely and positively and voluntarily, that the candidate speak a solemn vow, witnessed by a Beit Din—a vow that is the equivalent of *Lech L'cha*, an affirmation to leave "…*your land, your birthplace, your father's house…*" And that is what I did as I stepped into my mikvah, embraced by the warm waters of transition, to emerge as Tovah Miriam. *Lech L'cha* jumps off the page for me.

And here is a bit of real-life serendipity: *Lech L'cha* was the Torah portion that was being studied on the day I was born, October 15, 1945 or Cheshvan 8, 5706. *Lech L'cha* was to become the theme of my life. Its words were in the background, unbeknownst to me until very recently. And *Lech L'cha* resonates again with me now—loudly and clearly—now that I have left my land, my birthplace and, quite literally, my father's house.

Lech L'cha is the mitzvah of Jews in the diaspora and for any Jew who steps out of the waters of the mikvah, a stranger in a strange land. I did that. I left my land, that personal landscape of my childhood, with its quirky memories of going to the movies with my mother. I left my birthplace, my father's house—physically, metaphorically and truly. And my fainting in movie lines? Gone with the wind.

MAKING MY HEBREW NAMES

PATRONYMIC: *a name derived from that of the father or a paternal ancestor.*

HOW COULD YOU JOIN such a patriarchal system? Someone asked me this and I answer, Jewishly, a question with a question: How come you still call yourself by your father's name or your husband's father's name? We are all deeply enmeshed in a patriarchal system and we do not even notice it.

In 1969 I married a young man that I had met just one week after my mother died. By 1971 the marriage was over. It had been a mistake and, thankfully, our divorce would not cause too much harm.

When I sat in the attorney's office in 1971, in conference with my attorney and my husband's attorney over the terms of our divorce, I was told I would have to give up my credit cards and establish credit on my own after the divorce. In fact, I was instructed to cut in half my credit cards, in front of these witnesses, on that very day. Never mind that I had credit cards in my own married name and had always paid my own credit card bills on time—I was to cut up *my* credit cards on that day. My husband got to keep his.

In an added fillip of irony, I would soon find out that,when I went to rent an apartment, I would need the signature of a man to vouch for my credit-worthiness as a new renter. And so, my soon-to-be ex, agreed to sign for me when I got an apartment. He got the credit cards which he and I had established during our very brief marriage. I got his signature vouchsafing my trustworthiness.

I was steaming mad that day in the attorney's office, yet in a gauzy, sickening, mostly unconscious way. I was twenty-six at that time and decades would pass before I would be able to understand my anger over the particulars of my divorce in 1971. But in the moment of those events, all I felt was an as-yet unnamed hurt in reaction to the absurd legalistic instructions of that day. With my credit card shards on the table in front of me I blurted out,

—Well, can I at least have my name back?

In my marriage I had changed my maiden name to that of my husband's father, as was traditional in that era. And here's what the attorney for my husband said to me:

—Well, okay, but only if you don't use your name as an alias in committing a crime.

If I were to have committed a crime, it could well have been right then and there, I tell ya! Any jury would have understood.

And so I snatched back my patronymic to which I would fiercely cling for more than forty years. Through every job

and career advance, into a new and long marriage, onto
United States Treasury 1099 Tax forms, on driver's licenses,
insurance forms, doctor's workups, on the title page of my
single published book, I stuck to my own and only name,
an artifact of western culture, my patronymic.

It never occurred to me to take, for example, my mother's
maiden name which was, of course, simply her own
patronymic. Never even crossed my mind. And since all of
us women in my family line had taken the patronymics of
fathers and husbands, the taking of my mother's so-called
maiden name, would not have advanced the concept of
rejecting a patronymic. However, I did not know enough of
the world or think clearly enough at that moment to
discern the ins and outs of paternalism in our culture and
what it meant to me. For survival and for identity, I clung
tenaciously to my patronymic. It was mine, wasn't it? And,
leaving my early marriage, it was all that I had left.

Several decades later I became a Jew.

One of the most interesting things I was tasked to do before
dipping into the mikvah was to select my own Hebrew
name. Our rabbi advised the women in our group against
selecting the name of Ruth, as he said that that name would
be a dead-giveaway to being considered, always and forever
after, somehow other. Yes, Rabbi, but what about my given
name? Isn't Mary an unusual name for a Jew? I loved this
new assignment.

I wanted my new name to really be me, the person who I
had become over more than fifty years of living. I wanted

my new name to take me into the last years of my life as a symbol of both intrinsic, yet evolving, selfhood and my growth and evolution as a person, embracing and inter-weaving my secular self and my Jewish self. Without abandoning my old self, with its prominent and stubborn use of the patronymic, but in an act of weaving that old self with a new, and thus far, mysterious character, I wanted a name that embraced all of it, all of me, all of the aspects of me that I had been and that I would become. I wanted it to be my own name. I wanted to own and embody my new name.

And so I started with my given name and searched Hebrew naming dictionaries for a name which was equivalent to my given name or very similar to it; similar to my secular name, Mary. In addition to a linguistic pattern of sameness, I wanted a name which would symbolize my Jewish identity. Who had I become in the years that I had considered living Jewishly? What had I given and what had I received from my new identity? Well, certainly, as someone just beginning to embrace Judaism completely, I had taken more than I had given, so taking or embracing could be part of the connotations I hoped to find in my new Hebrew name.

Then I started thinking a lot about the concept of diving into the mikvah, and, as a non-swimmer, this last step in my commitment caused me a lot of anxiety. But in addition, diving into something had wonderful and positive connotations—as in diving into a stream of consciousness, into a pool of knowledge. Also, I had traveled on a long and sometimes precarious journey in joining the tribe. And there it was, a symbolism and linguistic similarity began to

merge into the Hebrew name I chose: Miriam. It was the
Hebrew equivalent to my secular name and it is a name
associated with waters and deep abundant wells and the
successful completion of a perilous journey. Miriam,
Moses's sister, was the one who always found the water for
the Israelites. She had a well that either traveled with her or
a well that she would find at each juncture of their forty
years in the desert. Wherever Miriam went, the well was
sure to go. I am reminded of the nursery rhyme, *Wherever
Mary went the lamb was sure to go* – a surprising allusion
to Christianity, I now realize.

There was one more step to take in my naming process. My
new name felt like it still needed something. To Miriam I
added Tovah, which means good. It was to be a reminder to
me to try to become a good Jew and to try to live up to my
chosen name of Miriam. So I put them together to make:
Tovah Miriam.

Words and names – only sounds, syllables, yes? Mantra?
My repetition of Tovah Miriam has become a mantra with
which I meditate on my changes, not necessarily in a seated
moment of meditation, but in the daily continuity practice
of meditation that I learned in Rabbi Cooper's classes.
Tovah Miriam is my mantra when I say my Hebrew name
to a friend, when I write it on an article, when I read it.

In addition to Judaism, I study Iyengar yoga. I see con-
nections to this ancient practice and to the antiquity of my
newly forming Jewish roots. I meditate and dive into my
mantra, my chosen names of Tovah Miriam. I repeat my
mantra, Tovah Miriam, and center on my heart, which

means I burrow into my heart, and I breathe in pranah, which means breath in yoga practice and, really, so much more than just breath. I slowly learn from repeating Tovah Miriam, as I release those words in a breath, a name—my new name—and by breathing it, Tovah Miriam can teach me who I am and who I am about to be. In this way my Hebrew name is taking root in me, is taking hold on the secular ground of a discarded patronymic habit.

How far have I come? Very far. How much did I leave? Not much: only everything.

Of course my secular name will be with me always; it will continue on legal documents, on checks, on the backs of credit cards. It will be on the front of this book. It will be with me always and will reside on my death certificate, with me, until death parts us.

My patronymic now preoccupies me. It is the name on my birth certificate and it makes official the man and woman who gave me life. But it no longer serves except as an artifact of a part of my identity, the identity I created in the first part of my lifetime. Now I am immersed, literally, in a new period of living. And more and more, my patronymic feels less and less like me.

What about a new last name? Though a Hebrew last name is not required at the moment of becoming Jewish, I am intrigued when Rabbi asks me,

—If you could choose any last name you wanted, what name would you choose?

Her question suggests another way to view my patronymic.
It is possible to change even that name. And so I start
another line of thinking. I am one who came as a stranger to
a strange land. I dove into the waters of another tradition,
even to the point of, quite literally, diving in over my head.

For a new last name I started with meanings first. There are
several web sites with Hebrew baby names and definitions.
I discover that there is a name for the stranger in a strange
land: Gershom. That's me. I am a stranger in this strange
land. And there is one more thing about the name Gershom
that further relates to Miriam. Gershom was the son of
Moses and Zipporah and Moses was Miriam's brother.
Can anything be better than that?

Tovah Miriam Gershom. And that is it. It is bashert.

—Ger Tzedek—

Converting Convert and Conversion

I HAVE A FRIEND, Joseph Cohen, who was born in Bulgaria and who became a United States citizen when he was thirty-five. He changed his entire life by studying US history and the Constitution and learning how Congress works and by learning what his responsibilities would be once he became a citizen. He studied for his citizenship simultaneously while working full-time as an accountant and while studying for his state certification as a CPA.

The ceremony for Joseph's citizenship was held at the convention center. There were 200 candidates in his class and they and their relatives and friends made up a huge crowd of more than a thousand people. Each candidate for citizenship held a little American flag. As the guests settled, a panel of judges and civic dignitaries entered the room and took their places on the dais. Then the candidates were asked to stand and to repeat after the Presiding Judge the *Oath of Citizenship of the United States of America*. It was silent in the huge hall as people who were born in France and England and Finland, and natives of Libya and Sweden and Russia and Bulgaria, and people from more than fifty other countries, recited the words in unison. No matter what your politics, it was a stunning moment. There were tears on the faces of the candidates, tears flowing down the cheeks of their loved ones. Then the last few words were spoken, "...*I take this obligation freely, without any mental reservation...so help me God.*"

A huge whoop went up in the room. All at once, people were jumping and screaming and hugging, and everyone, just everyone, was intensely, goofily, joyously, almost unbearably, happy, just happy and relieved and proud, ecstatic with physical emotional release. Then the Presiding Judge cleared his throat and said,

—Congratulations citizens of the United States!

He called them *citizens* and that was the actual moment of transformation.

Monumentally inspiring, Joseph Cohen! If you can do it, I can too. If you can change everything in your life, then here is the inspiration for me to do it too. I will study and work and learn my responsibilities and join in the Covenant and become a Jew.

And so I have done.

But there has been one significant difference for me from Joseph's experience. Following Joseph's ceremony of commitment to the United States, the judge called him a citizen. Following my commitment at the mikvah I was called a convert. Not by everyone, certainly, but by some. It is a title, a name, which can make me feel that I am somehow an outsider. It's a sticking point to my complete and joyful immersion into my new Jewish life.

Now to be fair, there are also other names for convert: *Jews by Choice* and *New Jew* for example. Yet, as sensitive as I am about the word *convert* I am as unhappy with its euphemisms. I have decided not to refer to myself by any of these names. Along the way, I have spent considerable time thinking about the effects of the word *convert* on me. I have given it a lot of thought, wondering why it affects me the way it does. Every time I hear it I mentally cringe. My conclusion has been that, within a Jewish context, the word carries with it many negative connotations. Bear with me while I explore this further.

A connotation is the suggestion of a meaning for a word apart from the thing it explicitly names. A connotation may be an idea or a concept or a pre-conceived notion that could be suggested by the mere mention of the word, aside from its singular meaning as a noun or a verb. Additional meanings may pop up in the mind of the listener who hears the word. And so the name, the word, *convert* has connotative baggage riding along with it. Say the word *convert* and a suggestion of meaning might form in a Jewish listener.

In the Jewish context, the verb *to convert* can suggest something dangerous, abhorrent, terrifying, as in the phrase: *convert or die*. Also, the name for one who does this thing, the *convert*, has negative connotations.

To be a Jew and to be forced to *convert* to another religion to be spared burning at the stake—this historic fact for

Jews in 1492 and at numerous other times as well—the word itself is ugly, perilous. You, the Jew, will be put to gruesome death if you do not *convert*. To be forced to *convert* loads the very word with horror. An atavistic shiver runs down the spine upon hearing those words: *conversion*, the action, or the verb to *convert*, or *convert*, the noun, the name for one who is forced to do this thing. Using this word to label or to name the person who converts to Judaism can bring with it subconscious and negative connotations.

And there is another layer of connotation to the noun *convert*.

To be a Jew and to acquiesce to your own *conversion*, to *convert*, the verb—even if you intend to secretly observe Shabbat, to secretly study Torah, to secretly remain a Jew—this is perhaps to die another kind of death. In your secrecy, you could die the slow death of the very real possibility of forgetting Jewish things, the slow death of suspicious neighbors peeking in your windows, the slow death from the fear that you will be discovered. This was the life for some *converts* who chose to hide in the lands of Crypto-Jewry.

I was an advertising copywriter during the classical age of *Meat and Potatoes* advertising, a decade after *Mad Men* and two decades before the Internet. As a copywriter, I wrote print, television and radio advertising. I was also required to name things. For example, a work order comes over the transom from management: What would you call a sandwich on a long bun with a wiener, mustard and relish?

Hot dog? Nah! That's already been done! Too boring! Back
you go, kiddo! We need a new name, something different
and sexy! That was my career for twenty years. Television,
radio and print advertising. And naming things.

Which brings me back to my current hobbyhorse: the use of
the word *convert* in my Jewish world. I am working on it
right now. The *convert* needs a new name.

I have heard *converts* say that they are *converts* in a variety
of contexts during Torah classes. Sometimes it has been
said as an excuse for not knowing something. Once or
twice I have heard a person use the word *convert* as a way
of drawing attention to the supposition that they know
more about the subject at hand than anyone else in the
room. Many times I have heard a *convert* saying that they
are a *Jew by choice* and I cannot understand why it would
have been necessary to say that in the context of whatever
the discussion had been. Often it's superfluous.

Yet there is this: Anybody who is a Jewish *convert* has had
to work hard to get there. Allow me for a moment to kvell.

For a *convert* to embrace Jewish life fully, they must enter
into that life with eyes wide open. A *convert* cannot act
precipitously, but must bring to the effort discernment and
thoughtful consideration and, I hesitate to use the cliché,
soul-searching. The *convert* cannot be merely a spiritual
tourist looking for a safe harbor. And, in fact, being Jewish
may not end up being such a safe harbor.

To *convert* you have to work. First to find a teacher. No

easy task when to even ask someone about entry into this Jewish world can be met with rejection. Tactfully or not so tactfully a candidate may be turned away several times. How does this work? There is writing required, writing about intentions before one even understands what, exactly, those intentions may be. Meetings with a rabbi to talk about – what? What kind of Jew you will be? Not an easy discussion when you have, at best, only a very hazy idea of who you will want to be Jewishly. There is a mikvah. Can you swim? And a Beit din? And it all culminates in a single sanctification in an affirmation ceremony.

All of this work and all of those hoops to jump through and you are called *convert*? You embrace the whole thing, warts and all, and what happens after the mikvah? Funny sideways glances at your new title: *convert*. Is this the only word to attach, for the rest of one's life, to such work? One might well feel like a second class citizen. Sadly, it is not true the playground chant: "*Sticks and stones will break my bones, but names can never hurt me.*"

On the contrary; names can hurt.

Well, there is always secrecy.

The *convert* keeps the *conversion* a secret and does not talk about it within the Jewish world. At the root of that secrecy might be this: if I say too much I will be rejected. So now this embryonic Jew feels fear of discovery and subsequent rejection. Sooner or later fear and secrets eat away at confidence.

But what about this example of naming: How about the symbolic and linguistic *conversion* of the bride? What I am talking about here is primarily the linguistic *conversion* of the word *bride* into the word *wife*. The bride makes a huge, sanctified affirmation during the ceremony of marriage and she is *converted* legally and metaphorically into a new person. She commits to work at this marriage for her lifetime. She makes many other pledges to her new life. Happily, she is *bride* for only a short time. She receives a new title that carries with it respect, reverence, love. Soon enough after her wedding she is forever-after: *wife*.

My friend Joseph Cohen made a solemn oath to "*...renounce and abjure all allegiance and fidelity to any foreign prince, potentate, state, or sovereignty, of whom or which I have heretofore been a subject or citizen...and that I take this obligation freely, without any mental reservation or purpose of evasion...so help me God.*" And within seconds the judge calls him *citizen*.

Beside the mikvah, I made a solemn oath and said,

*I make this affirmation as I enter the eternal covenant
between God and the Jewish people, the children of Israel.
I choose to become a Jew of my own free will.
I accept Judaism to the exclusion of all other religions,
faiths and practices and now pledge my loyalty to Judaism
and the Jewish people under all circumstances.*

*I promise to establish a Jewish home and participate
actively in the life of the Synagogue and the Jewish
community.*

*I commit myself to the pursuit of Torah and
Jewish knowledge.*

*If I am blessed with children, I will rear them as Jews...
Your people will be my people, and your God my God.*

And now I am called *convert*? That's it?

Can I change those old words which describe me as *convert*
and which sometimes name me *convert*? Can I apply my
old advertising self to the task of coming up with a new
name for this hotdog?

No.

Actually there is something much better. There is already a
name for this species of person. There is only one thing to
call this person and that name already exists.

Here is how it works:

There is only a single moment in time when a person must
be called a convert. It lasts for only a few seconds, only as
long as it takes a naked body to slide beneath the sparkling
waters of the mikvah. As head, arms, and every waving
strand of floating hair finds its way under the blue watery
surface of that small pool, then, and only then, and for
only that fleeting moment, a few seconds at most, for that
tiny moment of personal history, only then is that person a
convert. Because in the very next moments, seconds really,
as buoyancy overcomes the body after the third dip beneath
the waters of the mikvah, within mere seconds, as the

candidate pops back upwards, splashing and gasping to the surface and the waters stream back into the pool—then— then that person is a Jew. She is only the convert at one ineffable moment of sanctification and, bobbing to the surface of the waters of the mikvah, for now, and forever after, she is a Jew.

A Non-Swimmer Considers Her Mikvah

And then came my mikvah.

It was a requirement for my commitment to the continuity of Reform Judaism that I take a dip in the mikvah, an ancient symbolic ceremony which I would have to perform, in front of witnesses, as the sanctification of my decision. Along with the classes, the books, the study, the commitments and the solemn vows, Reform Judaism required that I had to immerse myself, alone and in nakedness, into a mikvah pool, not once, but three times, to dip my entire head under the water, hair and all, and to lift up my feet from the bottom of the pool and to float under the water in a physical act of the sanctification of my new life. Everything which preceded the mikvah was a pure joy—the study, the books, the classes. And I was certain about my decision as I have not been about many other things in my life. But the mikvah drove more terror into my heart than the contemplation of God. I could not swim. I was afraid of water. Here I was about to become a stranger in a strange land and now they wanted me to dip into a strange substance as well!

And so I began to prepare.

My studio sink is a couple of feet in depth and I filled it with warm water. The water was clear and warm and salubrious. I gamely dunked, face first, into its depths. My exhaled breath sent big bubbles past my ears and water filled my ear canals. Pool deafness again. It was not too bad, but my head popped up completely on its own as I experienced my own reflexes of bodily panic. I was panting, gasping a graceless slurp of air. Head dripping, heart beating erratically, I thought about it. It is not the lack of conscious fear, it is not the sincerity of my determination, it is the involuntary reaction of my own nervous system that performs what looks and feels like fear of the water. I attempt two more dunks, each one more ragged than the first.

What I discovered in my studio sink experiments was not that I was afraid of water, but that my nervous system was. In theory, I was not afraid of anything. And, specifically, I was not at all afraid of my decision to become Jewish. But my imagination of the water engulfing me, filling my eardrums, deafening and surrounding me, alone as I would have to be in the mikvah pool; I feared most a kind of incomprehensible claustrophobia. I feared that I might panic in a spasm of my autonomic nervous system's fear of drowning. My fear was once removed from my rational self and from my more spiritual soul, but I was actually controlled by the uncontrollable automaton of my synapses.

Rationally, I viewed the waters of the mikvah as a final test of my commitment to the Jewish people, to the generations

who came before me and with whom I was now committing
my soul to join. After all, they had endured much worse
than a pool of water.

Now the bargaining starts:

> Maybe I could take adult swimming lessons at
> the JCC.

> Maybe my Reform rabbi could give me a
> dispensation, after all we are Reform!

> Maybe Moses could do that water-parting business
> again.

I Google mikvah: 680,000 results in .08 seconds.

Almost nothing for the non-swimmer. This is too humiliating.

Fear and anxiety grow in me. Breathless, I am having a real
visceral anxiety attack. In feeling this anxiety, this beating
of my heart, this irrational mind-chatter, this escalation of
panic, I was experiencing my fear both in my head and in
my body. How can I be so ridiculous? Even I...I am
embarrassed by my own cowardly, growing, stupid fear.

In yoga there is a concept of understanding one's soul
through the careful observation of one's own body. By
paying minute attention to our body, we can learn things
about our mind, body, and soul. For example, by becoming
fully conscious of muscles that we grip, we can know two
things: 1) that we are, indeed, gripping them, and 2) that

certain tensed muscles indicate certain internal spiritual or psychological states. Dipping into my sink I gripped my stomach and violently gripped and flexed my arms and legs and my heart muscle pumped jaggedly—all of these bodily responses happened without being volitional. All were physical expressions of fear.

And then I started to feel something new. It seeped into me, a little bit at a time, each day in the days before my mikvah. Perhaps my fear of water had given me a unique insight into what it is to be Jewish. I could not have understood the all-encompassing bodily response of fear without my own feelings of fear of water. Has not fear been with the Jews for thousands of years? The jackboots in the night. The fires of hatred. The pogroms. The camps. Make no mistake: I do not mean to diminish or trivialize the historic fears of the Jews with comparison to my own small irrational fear of being out of my depth in the mikvah.

On the contrary. The instinctive fear in my own autonomic nervous system demonstrated to me, vividly and personally, exactly how much beyond rationality fear can be—how automatically our arms reach out for support, our lungs gasp for air—how the breath of fear subsumes all other rational notions of life. But, surely, if the Jews could live through that, and other horrors unimaginable, I can do this. If Jews have survived these horrors, profound, unutterable, unceasingly in their repetition over generations, and now ingrained into the Jewish psyche, then surely—surely!—I can take my little fears and bear them into the waters of my mikvah.

And so, the day of my mikvah arrives. Afraid of water or
not, today was the day I had to dive right in. Here I was
about to become a stranger in a strange land and off I
had to go into what was, for me, a very strange substance
indeed.

I will do this.

The water is warm and it sparkles in the clear morning
sunshine. My legs float out in front of me as the women of
my Beit Din murmur instructions and encouragement.
They ask me to close my eyes and visualize my life thus far.
I see my mother's smiling face. I see Aunt B.'s smiling face.
Their memories are, in this very moment, a blessing for me.
Then my Beit Din asks me to visualize my future life as a
Jewish person and I see a beautiful sunlit road winding into
a distant clear sunny horizon. My heart knows I am doing
the right thing. I feel up-lifted. I dip into the warm water,
face first, and feel—buoyancy!

I want to laugh. It is fine. I am fine. My hair floats for that
first dip. Three more dips will be required. It is fine. Each
dip is easier and more conscious than the one before.

Several things about the mikvah occur to me in these first
few weeks I spend as a Jew:

> The candidate has to go alone into the mikvah.
> This, I believe, is to ensure that I am acting by my
> own free will.

The mikvah ensures the embodiment of a soul's desire to "dive into" Judaism. It is not so easy to discern a soul during its transition into Judaism. But the Beit Din can see it in the quality of the dive under the water.

With the mikvah, I passed through one familiar earthly substance—water—and dove into a new and unfamiliar spiritual essence.

You have kept us alive that we might live to this day.

On my fourth dip I plunge in, almost euphoric. I open my eyes under the water, lift my feet and feel embraced and buoyed by the water as the mikvah waters support me. Uncertain now, of only one last thing—that it might not be okay to laugh, to giggle—I stand up on the floor of the mikvah, aware of the grace of this moment, wanting to laugh out loud with happiness. On my fourth dip into the mikvah I am buoyant and euphoric, almost laughing, feeling laughter with my joyous euphoria.

—Did I do it? Did I do it?

The women of my Beit Din were smiling,

—Yes, you did it! Yes!

To paraphrase: What makes this pool different?

When I stepped out of my mikvah, it was as if the San Fernando Valley swimming classes had happened to someone else. Which, in fact, they had done. This is the fact of my mikvah experience.

I walk in Mary and step out Miriam.

I did it!

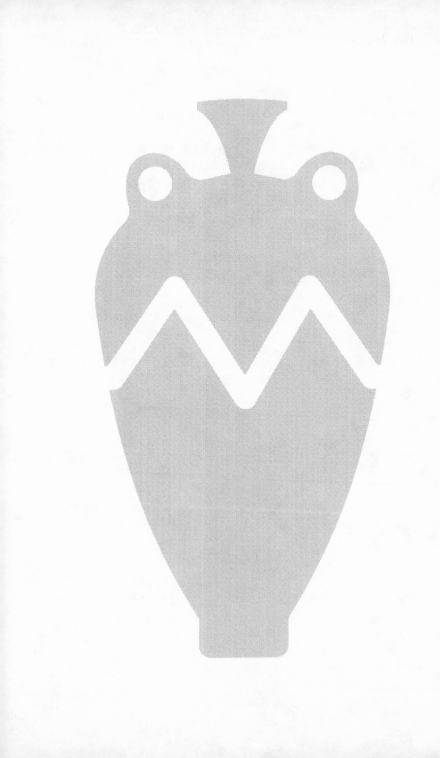

TIME

*The only reason for time is so that Everything
doesn't happen at once.*

—Albert Einstein

HE MUST HAVE STUDIED TALMUD. He surely studied Torah.

*God spoke to the Israelites and said, Not with you alone
do I seal this covenant, but with whoever is here, standing
with us today before the Almighty our God, and with
whoever is not here with us today.*
Deuteronomy 29:13

That's a lot of people standing around the mikvah waiting
for their moments in history to embrace the covenant.
Without the concept of time, everything is happening at
once. Everyone is joining the tribe at once. Think of the
multitudes!

Thousands at least. Millions more likely. Generations of
people from the past. And generations more, unknown at
this moment in the twenty-first century, but who are not
here today, but who will be standing there in the future.
Maybe billions of people comprise "*…whoever is not here
with us today.*" It is a mind-boggling concept that only an
Einstein could have begun to conceive of and what Einstein

did was to visualize all of these people together, in simultaneity, at a posited moment that would or could exist if there were no such thing as time.

Rabbi reminded me of this concept in an email discussion with me after my dip into the mikvah:

> *At the moment you came up from the waters of the mikvah, as far as the tradition is concerned, you, as I, stood at Sinai. Literally, and for real. But if you want to take that as poetry, try this because it isn't: At the moment you came up from the waters, all of Jewish history in one instant became your history, the same as if you were biologically born to it...Powerful stuff, all of this.*

Powerful, yes. And dizzying. Spinning in space and time, the continuity for the individual student who goes into the mikvah with a secular name, a secular mind, a secular self, inside a body existing in the twentieth century, all of Jewish continuity is embodied in a single naked human being and although that mikvah experience is only a small and private moment, imagine if time as we know it did not exist, imagine if everything were happening at once, imagine how crowded that mikvah would be!

Eons of time, throngs of naked souls crowding into and around that smallish pool, all of them committed to the covenant, and comprising those who are,

...not here with us today...

A very crowded moment indeed: women and men, Turks and Croats and Italians and Spanish and Portuguese, some French even, from the diasporas of Europe and South America and North America and some children, too, the children of parents who dip into the pool in continuity with the Israelites of Moses's time. People from centuries deep back into antiquity and people from eras unimaginable in unimaginable future times and spaces. People in colorful and splendid disarray and all of them dropping their robes at the edges of this single sparkling mikvah under the sun. Time, and the absence of time that only an Einstein could posit, time eradicated and just a jumble of naked bodies from a distant past—and including future people from who-knows-where—who will add to the continuity of the Jewish people because,

> *...The souls of all converts were also at Sinai...*

There we all were, and are, all of us, splashing into Einstein's theoretical pool where things happen all at once, a melee of arms and long shining hair, all trying to dip, one at a time and one after another, simultaneously in non-existent time, trying to dip completely, with no hair floating to the surface of the infinite water of this single mikvah, in a moment of,

> *...standing...today...with whoever is not here*
> *with us today.*

Breathtaking! Powerful stuff, indeed, Rabbi.

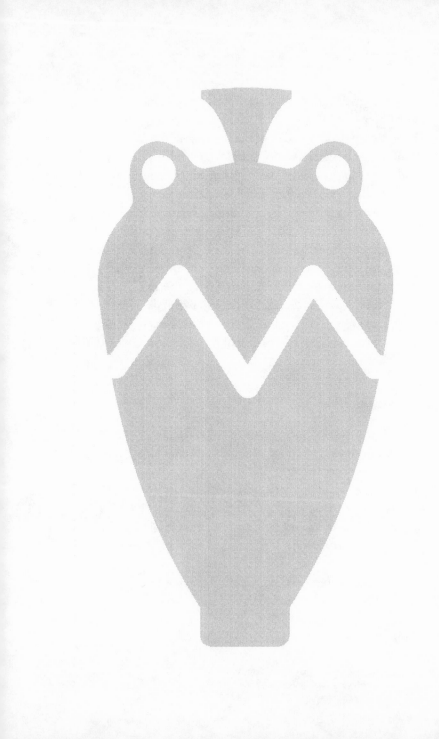

—Rosh Hashanah—

CHOPPED LIVER AND AMENDS

BACK IN 1993 I had a solo show of my paintings at a university art gallery. Entitled *Conceptual Portraiture*, the show consisted of about a dozen larger-than-life-size portraits of my dearest friends. Almost every person I had painted came to the reception and each one stood grinning next to their portrait for snapshots. Except for you, Aunt B. You hated your portrait and told me so.

Naturally I overreacted. I will never paint another portrait as long as I live!

Ten years later, around the High Holidays, I sit across the table from you at Junior's Deli in West L.A. We are happily dining on matzo ball soup and fragments of rye bread heaped with chopped liver. Your body is much shrunken because your spinal column has accordion-ed down upon itself for these past eight decades. Your head is just above table level. But you are bright and lively and alert and we are laughing. I push my soup spoon into the huge soft matzo ball, a dumpling really, and discover that it is surprisingly hot. Big shreds of chicken float around it in the bowl. You are tearing daintily with your perfect manicure and small long fingers at a piece of rye bread.

You seem preoccupied.

Then you say to me,

—You know that painting you did of me a few years back?

—Yeah, you hated it!

I concentrate on my matzo ball.

This is not an unfriendly exchange. I am reconciled now, and look up from my soup, a little teasing, and I see you across the table. You laugh a bit, tentative. You are, however, steadfast and I see that you are serious and want to say something more to me. Holding, in one hand, your shard of bread, and with your other hand in a fist, you gently thump at the front of your sweater.

Then you say to me,

—Well, maybe if I saw it again I'd like it better now.

You give me kindness and an olive branch and I take it, gratefully.

—Yes, I think you might.

Feeling clumsy, I smile then look away at all the families in this deli having pastrami and potato salad and egg creams and epiphanies. A rush of voices, all talking, talking, happy, angry, urgent, and some of it just quiet reconciliation. It is so clear.

To be completely truthful, I did not notice the gesture of
your hand, Aunt B., to your heart during that moment in
the deli. I noticed it, as a memory, after Yom Kippur
services, years later. My memory swept back to our meal in
the deli. Your gesture, small and subtle, hand to heart,
came into full focus long after you were no longer with us.
And, unbeknownst to yourself perhaps, or to me at the
time when you were doing it, you were communicating
something to me about how to be Jewish in the world.

—Yom Kippur—

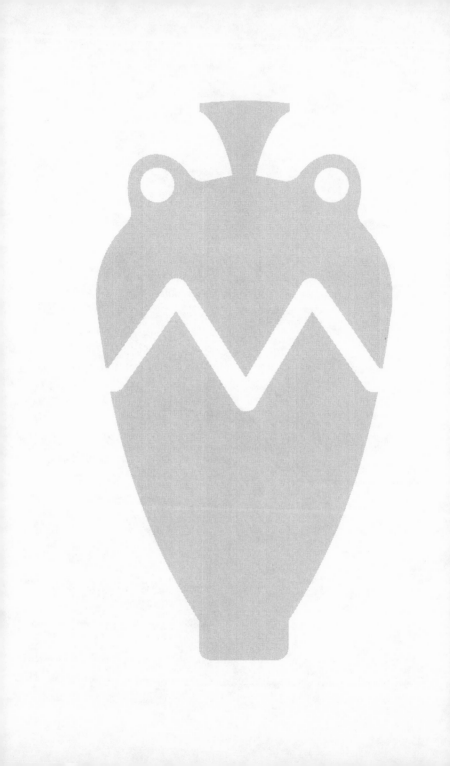

COYOTE

26 August 2013

ON MONDAY, as I rounded the corner of my studio with an armload of plant clippings, I was startled at the sight of a seemingly dead coyote lying on the sand near the pathway.

—Oh!

And then,

—What happened here?

I asked nobody. I asked the coyote.

Hearing me and seeing me, the coyote raised its snout, then its head and staggered to its feet. Thin and very wobbly, it stood there and we looked into each other's eyes. It was clean and thickly furred in the wild ochre tweed speckles of the desert floor. It was not bleeding or broken. It had a clean dry muzzle and stiff upright ears. It did not wretch or cough or make any sound whatsoever. There was no sign of sick on its hindquarters. The ground around it was clean and dry. The coyote was so weak and wobbly that it kept falling onto its side. Its legs were buckling as it tried to stand again and again and each time it toppled onto the sand again.

Gary had gone to the doctor, so I was alone at this point. I quickly dumped my garden cuttings and dashed back inside my studio to call a friend. He was unable to come over. He said to let nature take its course and that he would help us bury it later that day. They die too, he said, and I should just leave it alone.

Having witnessed many of my own pets dying, there was no mistaking this animal's last gestures. It was dying.

Right after the phone call I went back outside and discovered that, in the meantime, the coyote had apparently followed me around the corner of the building and back to the front of my studio. The coyote had hobbled along in my tracks, following me for more than fifty feet. It was lying collapsed again on the flagstone pathway that I had walked on when I went inside to make the call. It was lying now beneath my studio deck. It was breathing slowly and in regular breaths, not panting or gagging.

Several months later, I told our veterinarian about the coyote and he said,

—Dying wild animals do not follow human beings during their death throes. If anything, your coyote would have tried to hobble *away* from you, heading for a sheltering hiding place. I have never heard of a dying coyote following a human being down a path.

I watched it. It watched me. I discerned that it was either a half-grown pup or a female. It was small, but not puppyish, probably female. From time to time it staggered up, then flopped down again. It made a few wobbly steps to get under the deck. I turned on the hose which was a few feet away from it, but it seemed not to notice the trickle of water and made no attempt to get near the nozzle.

I felt that the right thing to do was to be with it and to stay with it until it died. It was minutes away.

Yet its eyes were still clear and seemed to look directly into my eyes. The eyes were not casting over as happens when an animal dies. After about forty-five minutes it was lying on its side and its head started to tip backwards—an unmistakable sign of dying which I have witnessed as our kitties died. Their neck muscles start to fail and the head goes backwards tipping onto the top of the animal's shoulder blades.

It wouldn't be long now.

Then Gary came home.

This coyote had followed me some sixty-five feet to lie down in front of my studio. And then it died.

Who shall live and who shall die?

(Note: Woven throughout these Coyote Diana essays, and appearing in italics, are lines from the Al Chet, which is the confession of sins recited ten times in the course of Yom Kippur services, and Unetanah Tokef, which is the central prayer of the Rosh Hashanah service.)

DIANA

30 August 2013

I WAS ABOUT TO LEAVE to go to Torah Study when the phone rang. Caller ID read *Los Angeles County Coroner's Office*. Gary answered the phone. I stood by with my bag on my shoulder.

After a few minutes hearing Gary responding with, yes, and yes, and then okay, he mouthed a name that we had not heard in thirty years. Then he hung up the phone.

—Diana?

—Yes.

—Dead?

—Murder.

Diana—Gary's first wife—had died on August 28, 2013, and the Coroner's Office was tracking down her next of kin. She died homeless, an alcoholic, on the streets of L.A. It was probably murder. The coroner said that there were no other next of kin. Gary, as Diana's ex-husband, was a kind of next of kin. In these first moments of learning of this sad event, we are almost without words. I ask what will become of her. Gary shrugs. We just stand there looking at each other.

Then I said,

—Let's give her a final resting place here in New Mexico. Call the coroner back and tell them we will provide a final resting place for her.

Gary calls the case worker back to start the process. The L.A. Superior Court requires a filing for an ex parte request to receive the remains. A judge must review the papers and sign off on the cremation and shipment of the ashes to another state.

We had not seen Diana for more than thirty years. Back then, she had had a pretty good job, living okay and, with luck, happily ever after.

We are shocked and much shaken by the news. It's worse than sad. I feel a sick clench of the belly, as if to avert a blow, except the blow had already struck.

The angels are dismayed.

The next day we contacted one of Diana's friends, Helen, who Gary had known from when he and Diana had been married. We had not spoken to Helen in almost forty years. She told us that Diana had been homeless for the past twenty years. In and out of rehab countless times. Hospitalized. Arrested. Jailed. Addicted to vodka. She stole money from friends. She stole a watch. She stole a car. She stole from an employer. She put the touch on everyone she knew and alienated all of her old friends over the years. We did not know any of this.

Who shall live and who shall die?

Then I realized that I had a role in this.

I began to remember a lot of things from my very brief acquaintance with Diana. And slowly I began to realize that I am, or was, culpable in her sad life and in her abrupt death. I began to feel guilty that I had been too forceful in saying to Gary that he could not give her any more money —that was back in the early-seventies after Gary and I had married. Diana had called often back then, asking him for thousands of dollars and he used to cough it up pretty regularly. The last time she asked him for money she wanted 5,000 dollars. Gary and I were both employed at big advertising agencies back then, we had double incomes, no kids. And I had said to Gary,

—Are you married to me or married to her?

I wanted Diana out.

…for the sin which we have committed before You by hard-heartedness…

And out she went. Again I remember saying to Gary,

—Are you married to her or married to me?

I am reminded of Sarah and Hagar. In my flailing despair and confusion I emailed the news of Diana's murder to a friend of mine, a rabbi, and he took gentle issue with my likening it to Sarah and Hagar and responded with this:

> —*Rather, it is that she, herself, didn't listen to the voice of the angel who said, Diana, what ails you? Open your eyes and see the well of water right beside you! Unfortunately, she didn't. Instead of providing herself with the salvation that was right there for her all along, she went the opposite direction. Tovah Miriam, read Gen. 21:19. It's all there. Only Diana didn't fill the water bottle. It wasn't yours to save her. It was hers to save her.*

When I heard his words, I was still not so sure.

I study Torah now in my retirement to discover how its ancient stories relate to my life, here and now. And the life story of Diana and my part in it reminds me of the story of Sarah and Hagar, and while I take the rabbi's point, my heart is not so sure. I still feel a hard, fearful thumping in my chest. Am I...was I...so innocent in Diana's story?

In the story of Sarah and Hagar there is an abuse of power. My stand against giving Diana more money was a power play by me over her. According to her lifelong best friend, Diana had wandered the streets of Santa Monica, combative, shouting, and addicted. I had a part in this. This I know. This I know now, now that I can look back through the tunnel of my life to a moment in time when I was cocky and hard-hearted. I, a young bright woman on her way up,

sentenced Diana with harsh words – she, a young lost
woman on her way down.

Who shall have rest and who shall wander?

If I had not been so set against Gary giving her any more
money maybe none of this would have happened. I am
culpable in some degree—and directly. Is that true? Or was
I just one of the straws that broke the camel's back, though
perhaps, not the last straw for Diana?

Now I *really* have something think about for making
amends on Yom Kippur 5774.

It was not really about the money—never only about
money. Money we had and potential. It was my own fear
that surfaced in every request she had made. I had felt
insecure in my new marriage to Gary. For years I never
really felt I was there in our life together and so I remained
on the *qui vivre*, ready in some background place of my
heart to leave and to again fend for myself, clever girl that I
had been, cocky, capable, easily employable, always with a
job, and, at bottom, untrusting.

And so when Diana called asking for money she was not
simply the ex-wife, she was a chilling portent of things
that I feared in my own life. I was selfish and hard-hearted.
After Gary and I married there was not a breath of com-
passion in me, back then, aged thirty or so.

Now, here it is nearing Rosh Hashanah 5774 and my friends
and confidants try to comfort me, to make excuses for my

behavior, as if it were some form of noble protection for my own marriage. I am not so sure I can rationalize my words from back then,

—Are you married to her or married to me?

I cannot rationalize. Words have consequences and, though late, my words echo back through thirty years of time and the words show up translated into the digitized message on caller ID: *Los Angeles County Coroner's Office.*

Who shall become rich and who shall be impoverished?

Diana died beaten in the street with nothing but her fingerprints.

We told the coroner that we will see to her remains and provide her with a final resting place. It is unlikely that any of her next of kin are still alive.

Who shall be at rest and who shall be tormented?

Too little. Too late.

My little excuses and rationalizations and even the rationalizations of my friends and of a rabbi, it all feels inadequate. Words have consequences.

LOW HIGH HOLY DAYS

CHRISTMAS IS THE HOLIDAY when everybody exchanges gifts. On Christmas Eve you hang your stocking by the chimney with care, and the Christmas tree is decorated and later that night reindeer, pulling a sled, clatter onto the rooftops and Santa Claus comes down the chimney and you've left a plate of cookies for him and he leaves tons of presents for you. Then, on Christmas Day your whole family comes over for Christmas dinner and there's a big fight and everybody goes home and says, "Whew! I'm sure glad *that* is over."

Whereas, for Yom Kippur we are to consider our shortcomings, to make amends with those we have injured throughout the past year and to contemplate death. We do these things while fasting. We fast for the whole day on this holy day. We are fasting when we consider the timeless question: *Who shall live and who shall die?* Finally, your whole family comes over to break the fast and there's a big fight and everybody goes home and says, "Whew! I'm sure glad *that* is over."

Joking is how I learn.

I mean no harm in wisecracking about both major religions. But truly, we Jews do the heavy lifting during our most solemn holy days. Confronting one's conscience is painful work if done in good conscience. Making amends in person, to those whom we have injured, is hard. Not hard. Excruciating. Excruciating and sometimes not possible at all. As when the person we harmed is dead. Especially excruciating when you are unaware that you even did the harm.

This is as much about fear as about regret. The regret is palpable—a sinking feeling in my chest and stomach, the same kind of lurching that one feels when the elevator in a tall building bounces and we react with visceral panicky fear that the elevator will free-fall. Fear is a huge component in the making of amends, not fear that one will be caught out in an act of treachery, but the fear that the very same act which we perpetrated upon another person will come home and be perpetrated against us. When I hear of Diana's homelessness and when I find myself at least partly culpable in it, I feel that lurch, that visceral panic in my stomach.

In this case, over the years I, and other women friends, have had a deep and irrational fear of falling—falling through the cracks and ending up on the streets, a bag lady with a shopping cart. I have one friend—a very smart and accomplished woman who was made the first woman vice-president at a very famous advertising agency—who spoke about her fears of ending like that. Through a haze of cigarette smoke, she'd mockingly joke about becoming a bag lady, clever little quips, and a bit too nervous. She seemed to believe that she, too, would end up on the streets. She even owned a shopping cart for a time and it sat parked in her breezeway at home to…to what…to remind her of this looming fate? To be prepared in case it actually came about?

Women in my generation often admit that we all came this close—with thumb and first finger measuring a very tiny distance—to losing it all. Even if I wanted to make amends for having a part in Diana's homelessness, it was too late. But the fear is immediate. My heart lurches. It is nauseating, my fear.

> *On Rosh Hashanah it is inscribed,*
> *And on Yom Kippur it is sealed…*
> *Who shall live and who shall die…*
> *Who shall perish by water and who by fire,*
> *Who by sword and…Who by famine…who by thirst,*
> *Who by earthquake…who by plague,*
> *Who by strangulation and who by stoning,*
> *Who shall have rest and who shall wander,*
> *Who shall be at peace…who shall be tormented…*
> *Who shall become rich and who shall be impoverished.*

This is all well and good and safe when repeated rhythmically, hypnotically, voices in unison, swaying, shuckeling, safe and warm in synagogue, safe from the intensity of these fierce words. And you are free from guilt, that kind of hot, visceral guilt of more personal guilt, because it's a poem, after all…and, well, it's just a poem. Maybe it's a prayer. And pretty soon you can break your fast with challah and smoked salmon and fruit.

In time for Rosh Hashanah and Yom Kippur 5774 we receive a call. The phone rings. Caller ID says *Los Angeles County Coroner's Office.*

A still small voice is heard...The angels are dismayed...

IN ANOTHER LIFE

I LIE IN MY HAMMOCK strung between two oak trees on the eastern slope of our acre in Northern California. Lying here I can see into the jaggy oak tree branches, high overhead, and swinging lethargically, with sunshine dodging in and out of the dry leaves, I feel an uncharacteristic warm breeze coming from the Bay. Behind my head, our hens mutter. On my elongated thigh-lap, one of our several cats stretches. Hovering above me, to my left, is our gorgeous, money sink of a house, our exasperating and beloved home. It looms overhead, quietly, secretly, treacherously rotting away with its next expensive surprise held in abeyance on this lovely, warm, calm summer day. It is a single moment of solitude. Bliss, if I were to name it. Gentle oblivion.

And Diana at that same moment? Snoozing on a bench in Santa Monica. Not a nice little restful snooze, but slumped, conked out, drunk, passed out, sprawling, unkempt, unwanted, in her tattered and makeshift garments, her tangled head lolls on a heart-shaped pillow. A tattered paper bag wrapped around a bottle? A dog? A dog, well cared for? Maybe if she had been lucky, she had a dog for her companion. The Santa Monica police note that often a homeless person's dog is better fed, better kept, than is the homeless person herself.

We had been so preoccupied in our lives back in the mid-
eighties and into the nineties. Back when Gary and I had
our own business, we pass many homeless souls on San
Francisco streets as we hurried to client meetings in the
towering One Sansome building. We brush rudely past
them, shouldering our Armani jackets and drawing our
pocketbooks closer to our chests as we pass them by. And,
although these people are shocking at times in their
dishevelment and delirium, they are not anybody to us.
They are nobody. The magnitude of it only dawns on me
now that I know a person's name, one of those homeless
people was someone we knew. Only we did not know it.
Back in Santa Monica at the same moments that we passed
by the homeless in San Francisco, that could have been
Diana.

A police report is part of Diana's L.A. Coroner's file. In
itself, as a document, as a last statement by a reliable police
officer—the report gives cold clarity to murder. The title on
the document is *Accident/Homicide*. As sub-text, a kind of
smug critical tone infuses that police report. The police
report says that among her possessions was a *soiled* sheet.
It's worse than criticism. It is pure mean lashon hara. Little
petit bourgeois cop!

What does "soiled" have to do with her humanity or to the
brutal manner of her death?

It was not a "soiled" sheet that killed her. It was a beating
at the hands another human being. And, how did you

decide that this beating was an accident? Her injuries were extensive, repeated blows to her entire body. The cop writes "soiled" into the last record of the human being who lies dead on the pavement and "soiled" becomes a word that will forever be associated with the end of her life? Soiled, he repeats, garments soiled, bedding soiled. You, a cop, you live in such pristine rooms that there is nothing "soiled" in your little home? You are such a clean upright individual that there is nothing "soiled" in your life?

What has "soiled" got to do with this dead woman's murder?

Well, perhaps I could justifiably say that it was a "dirty rotten murder." I could shout that couldn't I—with impotent rage to express my indignation at the word "soiled" in her police report. But as part of the record of a woman's murder, pointing out that her possessions were soiled carries no evidentiary weight. It matters little that this homeless soul possessed soiled items during the last moments of her life.

What if the dead person had been a rich *lady*—and I say lady intentionally in contrast to the homeless woman who had been Diana. For the rich victim of the same kind of crime, I suppose the cop might write, "She was draped in her *immaculate* silk scarf." Ask yourself this when you read that the homeless woman's possessions were "soiled."

What a dirty trick it is that the last words that record the death of a human being should include that her possessions were soiled. And what a dirty trick of fate that the cops drop the case and label it: *Accident/Homicide*. What does that mean? How can a homicide be an accident? Well, I suppose there could be accidental death resulting from numerous blows. Apparently there was no witness near the scene or nobody stepped forward if and when the police looked for clues. But she certainly did not just fall from a tree, as implied in the word accident. Not with injuries like those listed on this crime report. Play fair, you protectors of justice.

> *Justice, justice shall you pursue.*
> —Deuteronomy 16: 20

Well, let me amend that to read,

Justice, justice shall you pursue – for the rich, the note-worthy, the famous, the accomplished, and, might I add, for the *clean*—but as for the least among us, the widow, the orphan, case closed: *accident*. As far as for a homeless woman, a beating of that intensity is merely labeled: *accident*.

That's it? Case closed?

Ironic, that. Yes?

SHE DID NOT FALL OUT OF A TREE.
DO YOU HEAR ME!

The angels are dismayed...

THE POLICE DO NOT HAVE THE TIME or the personnel or the
political impetus or the rage of remaining family
members—or just what, exactly? What is it that they
require to pursue the murderer in this case? Looks to me
like nobody cares about the thin bony body that today
resides in the coroner's refrigeration unit.

But the court? Here's the irony. Nobody wants her. Nobody
will do justice to her case. *But.* The Los Angeles Superior
Court nonetheless requires a small mountain of paperwork
to give us permission to obtain her remains so that she can
rest, grounded at last in death as she had not been in life.
There would be quite a paper trail as Diana's remains
found their way into a small grave here in New Mexico.

Now that I take each High Holy Day more vividly into my
life, I am stopped short. This is excruciating. It is evident
to me this year, now, between the ringing of the telephone
with the call from the Coroner's Office and the sounding of
the ram's horn, nearing Yom Kippur 5774, I had a part to
play in this hard death. My own hard heartedness was just

one more thing that propelled her into her hard world.

For the mistakes we committed before You through having a hard heart. For the mistakes we committed before You through things we blurted out with our lips. For the mistake we committed before You through harsh speech. For the mistakes we committed before You by exercising power...against those who know, and those who do not know.

For the mistake we have committed before You through denial...through negative speech...by being arrogant... [by brazenness]...in throwing off the yoke, [refusing to accept responsibility] ...through jealousy... through confusion of the heart.

We have erred against You by hardening our hearts. speaking perversely...publicly and privately.

And this is it? This is all I can do, to write about my own struggles and about Diana's unknown struggles, as if it will matter? As if it will make a difference? As if to make amends? My words here carry a hollow ring.

We have erred against You by insincere confession, intentionally and unintentionally, knowingly and unknowingly. We have erred against You by perverting justice.

And when I said to Gary, "Are you married to me or married to her?"

… it is sealed.

Justice, Justice shall you pursue…

Otherwise telling Diana's story is mere voyeurism, self-serving insincere confession. Torah speaks to a passion for justice for the poor, the weak and the despised.

How do we…no…how do *I*, treat the weakest among us—the widow, the orphan? This self-examination at Yom Kippur has to be at the core of my Jewish identity. And what drives this self-examination has to be the finding of justice. Without pursuing justice this essay is just nicely crafted empty rhetoric.

Justice, how?

Justice, through what agency? The law? The courts? Through tearful prayer?

Justice? How can any of this be made right?

Well, of course it cannot be made right as she is dead already.

Please God, give her peace.

Well that's rich! Too little, too late!

Is this because I am Jewish? Why do I prod at these painful things? Maybe because I am new to this, this kind of rumination, this kind of conscience-work? Are the words of

Rosh Hashanah and Yom Kippur making new inroads into my conscience now? The words—they are so achingly powerful and if I really listen in full consciousness, what I hear, at this moment of my life, is a rebuke. No, this is not precisely what I feel. It's almost beyond my abilities to put into words how I feel.

Being Jewish includes the sanctification of daily life, all things sanctified, the challah, the studies, the murmur of leaves, the sanctification of food, of vows, of time, of a lifetime. This is hard. I want to dive into the clear waters of a clear conscience and I cannot.

Coyote. Diana.

Diana's death will be forever linked in my mind to that strange coyote death. Two days after the coyote staggered up the path, following in my footsteps to die, Diana died too. And the news of her death also followed me. The eerie simultaneity of the deaths links them in time. In coyote's death I am probably not culpable. In Diana's death I feel culpability. Is that the message I am meant to take from these deaths—that sometimes I am to blame and sometimes not? Is there a point to these deaths? I ask, *why*? There is no answer.

Maybe the better question should be, *And then what happened*?

Diana came to rest 21 November 2013 in Albuquerque, New Mexico. Nine people and a rabbi paid quiet attention to her life. I thank them here, with all my heart. May her memory be a blessing.

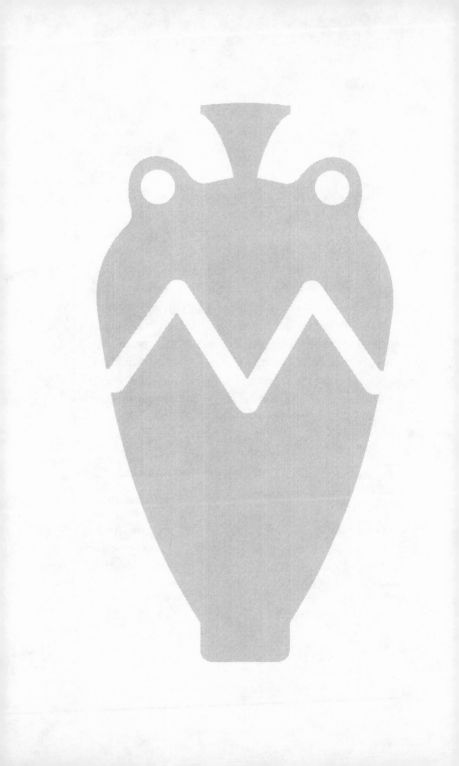

—Bashert—

FIGURE AND GROUND

—FUNNY KIND OF JEW.

This was my standard line after a social event or a dinner party where Gary had said,

—I'm Jewish.

He always said this when conversations turned to religion.

—Funny kind of Jew. You never do anything Jewish.

So when we moved from California to retire in New Mexico I was not really very surprised when Gary wanted to place a mezuzah on our front doorpost. While Gary's non-observance had not exactly changed into ritual-observance, it had, at least, become observable-observance, right there on the front of our new home.

Gary's Aunt B. said we were bashert. She came to this conclusion not simply because we had lived many decades of life together. She had what she believed was incontro-vertible evidence based on circumstantial evidence and intuition and she sealed her conviction with talismans.

More about that later.

Bashert: that lovely shushing Yiddish word that says you are fated, predestined. So Gary and I are predestined. I wonder if it is possible to be fated or predestined to something, or to some idea, that is not in human form? I mean, to being Jewish, for instance.

After my dip into the mikvah, I was asked, once and only once, and only by a single person: *Why?*

To which I could have said, with a shrug, Why ask *why?*

I am Jewish all right, answering a question with a question.

The man who asked me *why* was a retired surgeon. When he retired he started writing detective novels. I could as well have asked him the very same question: *Why? Why* did he go from surgery to detective novel writing? In fact, his shift in careers makes me ask, *why?*

I realize that questions are the tools of detective fiction. There is a dead body, still warm, on the hearthrug. And we, the reader, ask two important questions: *whodunit?* and *why?* These questions make a detective novel a compelling and juicy read. So then, not surprisingly, I am not surprised when this particular friend asks me *why?* But I suspect that my story is probably not as compelling and juicy as any of his detective novels. I wonder if I will ever be able to answer his question: *Why?*

Significantly, I believe, my teacher, my rabbi, who

supervised and advised and considered my decision to do this thing, this momentous move from one aspect of my life to another—even my rabbi did not ask me *why*? And Gary never asked me *why*? Rabbi, instead, asks me this interesting question: What do I intend to try to commit myself to in making this move? Rabbi asks me to tell him about my life thus far. Since I am over fifty years of age, that's a lot of narrative. Rabbi says to me,

—Being Jewish is not about belief. It is about action.

This I get. This I can believe. To *act*; this I can do. I understand action unequivocally, in my heart. And so, Rabbi asks me, what are you going to *do*?

But as for my friend who asks me *why*, I think maybe he needs a frame of reference for my decision to make this change in my life. He needs a plot. He finds my decision perhaps enigmatic, puzzling, a conundrum. In a certain mood, I might shoot back at him a wisecrack, "Well, *why not*!?" But I do not. I want to keep my friends, even if they ask me questions that I do not understand, that I cannot answer. I love my friends. So I begin to work with the *why*? of my friend, the retired surgeon-turned detective novelist. It rolls around in the back of my mind and I come up with commentary.

Reviewing what I have accomplished and how I did it, I see that it is not the entirety of details and characters from my life that have led me to the mikvah. It is, instead, a few precious details and people that have been most influential in my arriving at the moment of my mikvah. Certain moments and people and events do stand out—as figures stand out from ground in a work of art. They step forward in my memories, in my reverie, and there they are, standing alongside me at the mikvah pool.

So, if I am asked *why*, it is not so simple for me to create a single sentence to answer that tiny question, *why*? Maybe some things are simply, mysteriously, bashert.

UNCLES AND GRANDMAS

IN THE SUMMER OF 1945 my grandmother frets about the
worn-out old tires on her car. She's going to need good tires
to drive my mother and me to the hospital for my birth day.
It's still wartime and rubber tires are rationed, virtually
impossible to find. But she gets new tires, or at least tires
as-good-as, when she buys old re-grooved tires on the black
market. Grandma Zimmerman tells me the story over and
over again during my growing up, so I remember it.
Grandma tells me that she bought the black market tires
from,

—That Jew over on the west side.

I cringe to remember Grandma's casual anti-Semitism.
I am ashamed. It hurts my heart that my beloved grandmother could sound so coarse and mean and that this
bright woman could be so ignorant. Happily, surprisingly,
her ugly attitude did not rub off on me. But to apologize
for it cannot make up for it. Excuses will not expunge her
ignorance, her cruelty. That it was the attitude of the day in
that wartime era, does not change how I feel as I remember
it. I am ashamed. And this was the same grandmother who
took my childhood artistic attempts and my teenage
lonesome poems very seriously.

—You have the hands of an artist.

She told me this, several times, and I have treasured her for that ever since.

But decades later, her story about the re-grooved tires was to become the suggestive hook, the real-life coincidence, which seemed to predestine Gary and me. Many decades later Gary's uncle, a compelling raconteur, told us his famous story and we were to discover, through Aunt B., that it related to my grandma's re-grooved tire story.

Here is how this played out:

Gary's uncle recounts the apocryphal family story of how he bought their big house in Beverly Hills. Back in the fifties in Beverly Hills, Gary's uncle was looking at a house that was for sale on Sunset. During the tour of the rooms, the owner of the house said to Gary's uncle that he'd sell him the house for less than he was offered by another man who was a *Jew*. This was the same smug anti-Semitism of the era, the same words that my grandmother had used to describe the man who sold her regrooved tires back in 1945. Only this time it's Gary's uncle who's telling the story about himself and he's laughing. He's laughing because the owner of the house did not realize that Gary's uncle was Jewish too. Gary's uncle bought the house. He was pleased with himself for putting one over on the guy. A Jew bought the house anyway!

Then Gary's uncle told us that during the war he had sold re-grooved black-market tires over on the west side. It had to have been from him that Grandma purchased those tires in 1945. And the thing that brought these two disparate family stories into focus for Gary and me was the casual anti-Semitic attitudes of the era.

I will always feel shame remembering my part of the family story. Grandma's language was a shanda. But Gary's uncle laughs recounting his part of the story. Laughs. I am surprised by his apparent glee in telling us the story about the guy who didn't want to sell the house to a Jew. Gary's uncle showed easy grace and bantering laughter with only a tiny bitter shrug of resignation. There was anger there, but much louder was his laughter. In fact his laughter was so infectious that we were all laughing by the end of the story. Jewish humor in real life!

And here is the real capper: Fifty years after the tires and the real estate deal, our Aunt B. deduced that those two family stories were incontrovertible coincidence and, as such, they were incontrovertible evidence that Gary and I were bashert. She believed wholeheartedly that my grandmother and Gary's uncle had met before I was born. What that meant was that Gary and I were bashert. Had it not been for Gary's uncle's regrooved tires, and the fact that my grandmother purchased those tires from him, my mother might not have gotten to the hospital safely when she was in labor with me. The world is a wondrous and mysterious place!

Soon after the family stories came to light, our aunt gave Gary and me Mizpahs. A Mizpah is a bond between people who are separated, either physically or by death. And

Mizpah jewelry is worn to signify this bond. The jewelry that she gave us was a single medallion and two chains. The medallion has the word Mizpah on the front and on the back this verse from Torah, Genesis 31:49:

> *And Mizpah; for he said, The Lord watch between me*
> *and thee, when we are absent one from another.*

Down the middle of the medallion was an incised broken line and we were to each hold one side and to break it in half. We each placed our half medallion on a chain to wear around our neck when we were to be apart. The odd part was that, at that point in our lives, Gary and I had a business together and we were rarely apart. But we wore them anyway and still do from time to time.

Bashert we were in the eyes of Gary's Aunt B. and bashert we would always be.

It's complicated. Out of something shameful comes something good. What a gift our aunt created with the juxtaposition of these family stories. She softened the ugly language and came to a new conclusion: bashert. Gary and I were bashert. May her memory be a blessing.

BASHERT

IN YIDDISH *bashert* means to be *destined*. As I see it, I
believe that it may work like this: Things or events in time
bump up against each other to affect the outcome of other
things or events in the future. Turn the kaleidoscope and a
blue piece and a red piece bump randomly up against each
other for the first time and something new is revealed by
their proximity. Coincidence can show you a glimpse of
your own destiny.

Albert Einstein observed that,

> *Coincidence is God's way of remaining anonymous.*

So what about free will? Jews believe that we have free will.
That means that if coincidence presents us with a glimpse
of possibility, we are free to say yes or no to it. In my
lifetime I have received and acted upon many coincidences,
many moments of destiny—or of predestination. It could
be comforting to believe that someone or something is
guiding me, guiding me as I live my life, giving me a nudge
here and a wink there.

And now, I do, often, reflect on intersections of events in
my own life.

Bashert could be that little girl reading comic books and Walden. Bashert could be Anne Frank speaking to me from history. Bashert might have been Francoise Sagan whispering to me about charming imperfect fathers. Bashert may have been my mother, the gunnery instructor, and her fierce warrior love converging across the badminton net. Bashert may well have been my raucous ignorant brilliant grandmother swearing at the gardener and everybody else in the world. Bashert may have been my Zimmermans, *Those Zimmermans*, fleeing their own heritage to change everything about themselves. Bashert could be hidden in *Parsha L'ech L'cha*, hovering over my birthdays, and waiting for me to take notice someday. And maybe that little girl playing TV commercials is bashert. Maybe when the student is ready, the teacher will come is bashert.

Bashert kept popping up over the years, the decades, in my life. Bashert keeps happening even now. It's corny, sure. And maybe it's really true.

I note that as bashert as Gary and I are, I am as bashert now about being a Jew. This thing happens and then that thing happens and then what happens next? What happened to me next seems to have always been bashert. But action was always required on my part—action to pay off the coincidences of bashert.

The covenant is sealed with those who are here today and those who are not here today. My mother dies. Intuitively I make yahrzeits for her. I marry into a Jewish family. I have a Eureka moment. I find my teachers. They find me. I discover my names. I plunge into the mikvah. Being Jewish is not about belief. It's about action.

I embrace my Jewish life.

My Jewish life embraces me and now I can recite:

> *Barukh ata adonai eloheinu melekh ha'olam, she-he-*
> *ch'yanu, v'kiyemanu, v'higgianu lazman hazeh.*

This is the Jewish prayer of gratitude:

You abound in blessings, Eternal One our God, Sovereign
of all time and space, who has kept us in life, sustained us
and allowed us to reach this moment.

L'Chaim!

To Life!

AFTERWORD

WE HAVE A FRIEND, *Jewish-born, and a person who is the relative of a very dear friend of ours. We see this friend from time to time. He is our age, which means that he has grown children and some grandchildren. Over dinner tables, when we have talked about being Jewish in the world, he has spoken of his disaffection with being Jewish. He has told us about an episode with a rabbi over a bar mitzvah and he has said that it's one of the many reasons that he feels disaffected from being Jewish. Gary admires anyone who can hold a grudge for more than forty years and so we end up really liking him.*

At Chanukkah, that first year after my Simchat Mikvah, I made a party in our home and invited a minion of close friends which included this man. In the pre-dinner hoopla, with everyone noshing and talking and laughing, he spoke quietly to me and said,

—I really admire and respect what you did. They do not make it easy do they? And I just want you to know that I admire the fact that you saw it through and that you did it.

He spoke quietly in the din of the room, not drawing attention to our private conversation and he gave me this grace in a brief and full-hearted way and all I could say was,

—Thank you.

There was so much more I wanted to say, but could not at that moment. Maybe if he reads this book he'll recognize himself at this Chanukkah party.

As I said when I began this story: How I made my Simchat Mikvah is contained in the kaleidoscope of my life events, all jumbled together.

Turn the kaleidoscope, either clockwise or counterclock- wise, and move forward or backward in time. Someone from my past bumps into someone I met last week. Something I learned in childhood bumps into something I Googled yesterday.

The kaleidoscope, however, stops at the edge of the mikvah. For a few sanctified seconds, the bits and pieces stop tumbling and loved ones and cherished events and sad things and mad moments and sense and nonsense and the whole shifting content of a lifetime come to rest. The pieces come to rest at the side of this pool. After my mikvah, the kaleidoscope starts to turn again and new pieces will be added.

The question throughout this book has been: And then what happened?

Now the question changes: And now what happens?

ACKNOWLEDGEMENTS

THREE RABBIS were my first teachers. Two women attended as members of my Beit Din, offering me wise counsel and they were also witness to my immersions during my Simchat Mikvah. May all of them live to be one hundred and twenty. These rabbis and these wise women are imprinted with love upon my heart, forever

This book has taken more than five years to write and has its roots in a Jewish meditation retreat that I attended in 1996.

Thank you to Sharon Baker and Julie Denison who listened to some of these stories as I read aloud to them. Their enthusiasm encouraged me to continue.

Thank you, dear friend, Norma Libman, for all your work and attention as my literary, cultural and always supportive advisor throughout the entire project.

First readers of the completed manuscript include Irene Seff, Tammy Kaiser and Liz DuFrane. Their discerning attention and subsequent encouragement meant the world to me.

My editor, Ann Paden, has proven to me, again, that some things are, indeed, bashert; thank you Ann.

Friends who knew about my progress and who were warmly enthusiastic when I became a Jew are integral to my story. Nancie and Sandy Gilbert, Barb Wexler and Sondra Birkenes, Amy Libman Cohen and Joseph Cohen, Laura Scheflow, Allison Smith, and Jody Legendre Weiskopf. And special thanks to Joseph Cohen for allowing me to include an essay on his becoming a United States citizen.

For the regulars in the Friday class *Torah and Beyond*, at Congregation Nahalat Shalom, which I have attended since 2012—Tova Indritz, David Nachumson, Irene Seff, Shad Goldstein, and Joan Robins: You inspire, instruct, and provide support as I discover how to be Jewish in my world.

For my friend, surgeon and detective novel writer, C. Francis Roe, thank you for asking the question which nudged me to think more deeply about *why*.

I am thankful that my mother Mary, my mother-in-law Annette, and our Aunt Bea still feel close to me today. And thanks to my grandmother Jennie and Gary's Uncle Martin for the varieties of strength that they imbued in me. All of their memories are a constant blessing.

For the immediate future of my Jewish life, I thank Deborah Gullo, my yoga teacher, for breathing life into our Torah Yoga Workshop.

For my husband Gary, inexpressible love and gratitude are entwined round our daily lives of more than forty years together.

L'Chaim!

—Mary E. Carter/Tovah Miriam Gershom 2014

Photo: Gary W. Priester

About the Type

Sabon is an old style serif typeface designed by the German-born typographer and designer Jan Tschichold (1902–1974) in the period 1964–1967. The typeface was released jointly by the Linotype, Monotype, and Stempel type foundries in 1967.

Tschichold lived in Leipzig and in the 1920s had devised a "universal alphabet" for German, improving its non-phonetic spellings and promoting the replacement of the jumble of fonts with a simple sans serif. He was a modernist, and after the war, from 1947 to 1949, played a hugely significant role in British book design, creating timeless modern layouts and fonts for Penguin Books. For the German printers, he crafted Sabon as a font that modernized the classics and honed each letter's fine details, particularly the evenness of the serifs.

Design of the roman is based on types by Claude Garamond (c.1480–1561), particularly a specimen printed by the Frankfurt printer Konrad Berner. Berner had married the widow of a fellow printer Jacques Sabon, the source of the face's name. The italics are based on types designed by a contemporary of Garamond's, Robert Granjon. The typeface is frequently described as a Garamond revival.

From Wikipedia, the free encyclopedia

ISBN 978-0-692-26582-6

51500>

9 780692 265826

A Non-Swimmer Considers Her Mikvah
On Becoming Jewish After Fifty - Essays
By Mary E. Carter